LIFT IT, PUSH IT, PULL IT

McGRAW-HILL
SCIENCE

MACMILLAN/McGRAW-HILL EDITION

LIFT IT, PUSH IT, PULL IT

RICHARD MOYER ■ **LUCY DANIEL** ■ **JAY HACKETT**
PRENTICE BAPTISTE ■ **PAMELA STRYKER** ■ **JOANNE VASQUEZ**

NATIONAL GEOGRAPHIC SOCIETY

McGraw-Hill School Division

New York — Farmington

Program Authors

Dr. Lucy H. Daniel
Teacher, Consultant
Rutherford County Schools,
North Carolina

Dr. Jay Hackett
Emeritus Professor of Earth Sciences
University of Northern Colorado

Dr. Richard H. Moyer
Professor of Science Education
University of Michigan-Dearborn

Dr. H. Prentice Baptiste
Professor of Curriculum and Instruction
New Mexico State University

Pamela Stryker, M.Ed.
Elementary Educator and Science Consultant
Eanes Independent School District
Austin, Texas

JoAnne Vasquez, M.Ed.
Elementary Science Education Specialist
Mesa Public Schools, Arizona
NSTA President 1996–1997

NATIONAL GEOGRAPHIC SOCIETY
Washington, D.C.

Contributing Authors

Dr. Thomas Custer
Dr. James Flood
Dr. Diane Lapp
Doug Llewellyn
Dorothy Reid
Dr. Donald M. Silver

Consultants

Dr. Danny J. Ballard
Dr. Carol Baskin
Dr. Bonnie Buratti
Dr. Suellen Cabe
Dr. Shawn Carlson
Dr. Thomas A. Davies
Dr. Marie DiBerardino
Dr. R. E. Duhrkopf
Dr. Ed Geary
Dr. Susan C. Giarratano-Russell
Dr. Karen Kwitter
Dr. Donna Lloyd-Kolkin
Ericka Lochner, RN
Donna Harrell Lubcker
Dr. Dennis L. Nelson
Dr. Fred S. Sack
Dr. Martin VanDyke
Dr. E. Peter Volpe
Dr. Josephine Davis Wallace
Dr. Joe Yelderman

Invitation to Science, *World of Science*, and *FUNtastic Facts* features found in this textbook were designed and developed by the National Geographic Society's Education Division.
Copyright © 2000 National Geographic Society
The name "National Geographic Society" and the Yellow Border Rectangle are trademarks of the Society, and their use, without prior written permission, is strictly prohibited.

Cover Photo: ZEFA/Stock Imagery, Inc.

RFB&D
learning through listening

Students with print disabilities may be eligible to obtain an accessible, audio version of the pupil edition of this textbook. Please call Recording for the Blind & Dyslexic at 1-800-221-4792 for complete information.

McGraw-Hill School Division
A Division of The McGraw-Hill Companies

Copyright © 2000 McGraw-Hill School Division,
a Division of the Educational and Professional
Publishing Group of The McGraw-Hill Companies, Inc.

All rights reserved. No part of this book may be reproduced or transmitted in any form or by any means, electronic or mechanical, including photocopying, recording, or by any information storage and retrieval system, without permission in writing from the publisher.

McGraw-Hill School Division, Two Penn Plaza, New York, New York 10121

Printed in the United States of America

ISBN 0-02-278207-9 / 3

4 5 6 7 8 9 058/046 05 04 03 02

CONTENTS

UNIT 2 — LIFT IT, PUSH IT, PULL IT
PHYSICAL SCIENCE

CHAPTER 3 • HOW THINGS MOVE 65

Topic 1: ON THE MOVE! 66
- **EXPLORE ACTIVITY** Investigate How Things Move 67
- **QUICK LAB** Picture the Position 69
- **NATIONAL GEOGRAPHIC WORLD OF SCIENCE**
  Are We There Yet? 74

Topic 2: PUSHES AND PULLS 76
- **EXPLORE ACTIVITY** Investigate Why Some Objects Are Harder to Pull 77
- **SKILL BUILDER** Interpreting Data: Reading a Bar Graph 82
- **SCIENCE MAGAZINE** Show Your Muscles! 84

Topic 3: FORCES IN MOTION 86
- **EXPLORE ACTIVITY** Investigate What Causes a Change in Motion 87
- **QUICK LAB** Marbles in Motion 92
- **SCIENCE MAGAZINE** Dancing on Rocks 94

CHAPTER 3 REVIEW/PROBLEMS AND PUZZLES 96

CHAPTER 4 • WORK AND MACHINES 97

Topic 4: DOING WORK 98
- **EXPLORE ACTIVITY** Investigate What Work Is 99
- **QUICK LAB** Changing Energy 101
- **SCIENCE MAGAZINE** Earth at Work 104

Topic 5: GETTING WORK DONE 106
- **DESIGN YOUR OWN EXPERIMENT** How Can You Make Work Easier? 107
- **QUICK LAB** Make a Lever 110
- **SCIENCE MAGAZINE** A Music Machine 114

Topic 6: MORE SIMPLE MACHINES 116
- **EXPLORE ACTIVITY** Investigate How a Ramp Can Make Work Easier 117
- **SKILL BUILDER** Using Numbers: Evaluating Differences 121
- **SCIENCE MAGAZINE** Simple Machines on a Playground 124

CHAPTER 4 REVIEW/PROBLEMS AND PUZZLES 125
UNIT 2 REVIEW/PROBLEMS AND PUZZLES 126–128

REFERENCE SECTION

HANDBOOK R1
    MEASUREMENTS R2–R3
    SAFETY R4–R5
    COLLECT DATA R6–R10
    MAKE MEASUREMENTS R11–R17
    MAKE OBSERVATIONS R18–R19
    REPRESENT DATA R20–R23
    USE TECHNOLOGY R24–R26

GLOSSARY R27

INDEX R39

UNIT 2
LIFT IT, PUSH IT, PULL IT

CHAPTER 3
HOW THINGS MOVE

What makes something move? Why do some things move faster than others? What makes an object stop moving?

In Chapter 3, you will read several diagrams. A diagram uses pictures and words to show how something works.

Topic 1
PHYSICAL SCIENCE

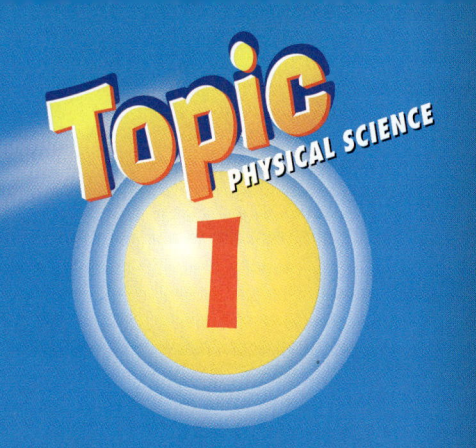

WHY IT MATTERS

All around you, things are always moving.

SCIENCE WORDS

position the location of an object

motion a change of position

speed how fast an object moves

On the Move!

The Circus Is in Town

The circus is in town!
The circus is in town!
Here come the tigers.
Here comes the clown.
Here come the fliers
On the trapeze
Soaring through the air,
Hanging by their knees

Jugglers, dancers,
Twirling acrobats
Dangerous animals,
Balancing acts.
Up on the tight rope,
Far from the ground
Don't look now—
The circus is in town!

• • • • • •

Who do you think moves faster—the tightrope walker or the acrobats? How do you know?

EXPLORE

HYPOTHESIZE How much faster do you run than walk? Write a hypothesis in your *Science Journal*. How might you test your ideas?

66

EXPLORE ACTIVITY

Investigate How Things Move

Compare the time it takes you to run a certain distance with the time it takes you to walk that same distance.

MATERIALS
- stopwatch
- 1 red crayon
- 1 blue crayon
- graph paper
- meter tape
- *Science Journal*

PROCEDURES

1. **PREDICT** Look at a distance of 10 meters. How long will it take you to run 10 meters? How long will it take you to walk 10 meters? Record your predictions in your *Science Journal*.

2. **MEASURE** Use the stopwatch to time how long it takes each person in your group to run 10 meters. Record each person's time.

3. **MEASURE** Time how long it takes each person in your group to walk 10 meters. Record each person's time.

CONCLUDE AND APPLY

1. **COMPARE** Look at your predictions of how long it would take you to walk and run 10 meters. How do they compare to the times you measured?

2. **COMMUNICATE** Print each person's name on a line at the bottom of the graph paper. Use a red crayon to mark an X above your name to show how many seconds it took to walk 10 meters. Use a blue crayon to mark an X that shows how many seconds it took to run 10 meters.

3. **INTERPRET DATA** What is the difference, in seconds, between your times for walking and running?

GOING FURTHER: Problem Solving

4. **PREDICT** Use your graph to predict how long it would take you to walk 20 meters.

67

How Do Things Move?

You've just seen many different types of movement. In the circus on page 66, tigers roared while acrobats soared. The Explore Activity shows that you can move in different ways, too. What are some different ways that you move?

How do you know an object is moving? Take a look at the toy cars in picture A. Do either of them seem to be moving? How can you tell?

A The Start

Start   **Finish**

Now look at picture B. Ten seconds have passed. The blue car seems to have moved because it changed **position** (pə zish′ ən). What is position? To find out, keep reading.

B 10 Seconds later

Start   **Finish**

Position is the location of an object. Everything has a position. Your nose has a position in the middle of your face. The red car has a position at the starting line.

Some positions change. The blue car moves from the starting line to the finish line. Other positions don't change. Your nose stays in the middle of your face. The red car stays at the starting line.

How do you describe an object's position? You can compare it to the positions of other objects. Special words like *above* and *below*, *left* and *right*, *ahead* and *behind* give you clues about position. The pink fish is above the green fish. The yellow fish is behind the pink fish. The green fish is ahead of the yellow fish.

Which fish are above? Which are below?

QUICK LAB

Picture the Position

HYPOTHESIZE Do position words help you give directions? Write a hypothesis in your *Science Journal*.

PROCEDURES

1. Sit opposite your partner at a table. Prop up the notebook between you. Create a building with your blocks.

2. **COMMUNICATE** By describing the position of each of your blocks, instruct your partner to create the same building.

3. **COMPARE** Remove the notebook. Are the buildings the same? Switch roles and try it again.

MATERIALS
- 2 sets of 5–7 blocks
- a notebook
- *Science Journal*

CONCLUDE AND APPLY

DRAW CONCLUSIONS What would happen if your partner gave you directions without using position words? Could you still build the building?

69

What Happens When an Object Changes Position?

Think back to the toy cars on page 68. You knew the blue car moved because it changed position. When an object changes position, the object is in **motion** (mō'shən). Motion is a change of position.

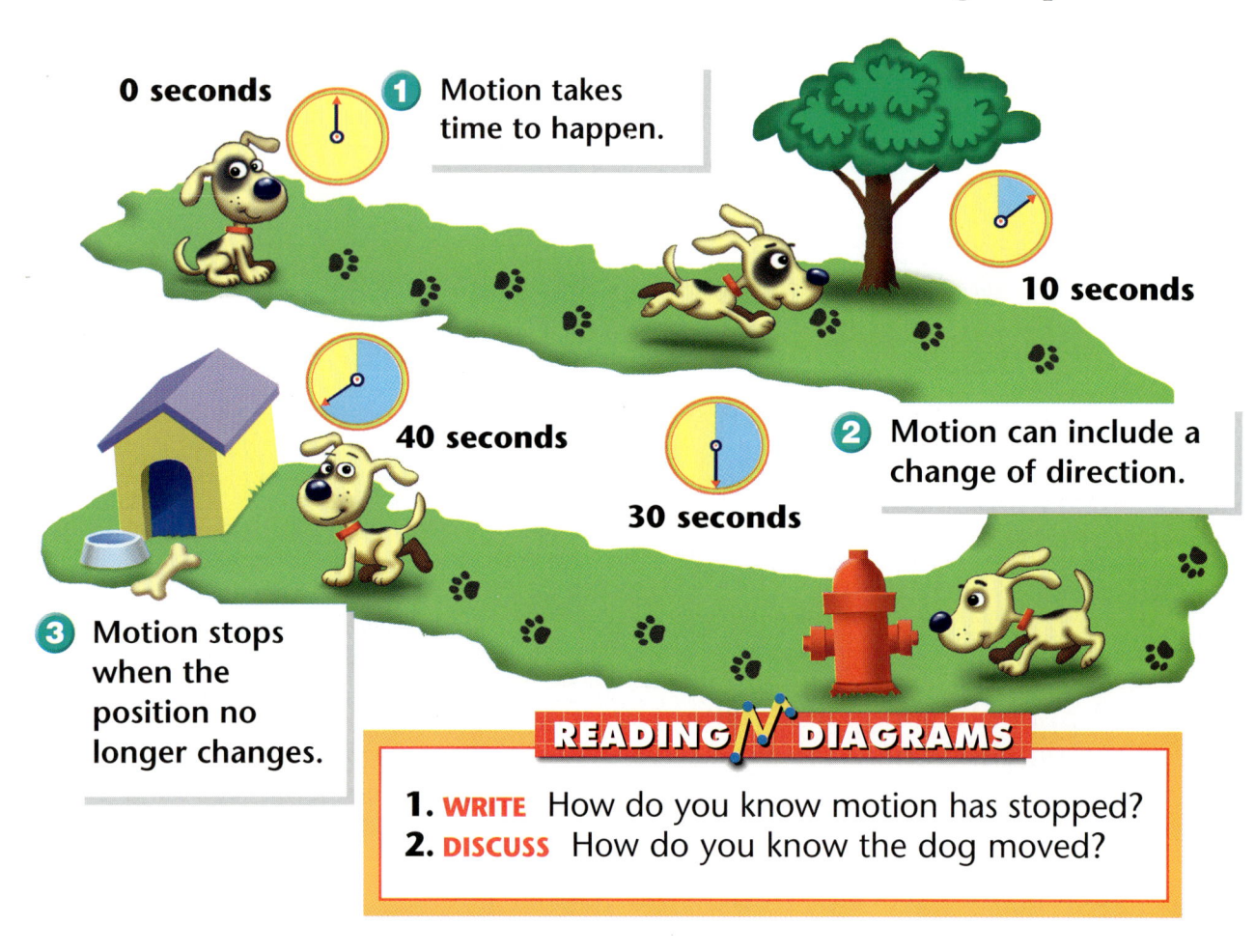

0 seconds

1 Motion takes time to happen.

10 seconds

40 seconds

30 seconds

2 Motion can include a change of direction.

3 Motion stops when the position no longer changes.

READING DIAGRAMS

1. **WRITE** How do you know motion has stopped?
2. **DISCUSS** How do you know the dog moved?

Some motions are hard to see. The ball is kicked so hard that it looks like a blur. The snail moves so slowly that it doesn't seem to be moving. What is the difference between these two motions? One happens very fast. One happens very slowly.

The snail moves slowly.

The ball is moving quickly.

70

How Fast Do You Go?

Some things move faster than others. Things that move faster have a greater **speed**. Speed is how fast an object moves. You can judge an object's speed by how quickly it changes position. A fast-moving object changes position quickly. A slow-moving object takes longer to change position.

How do you measure speed? You need to measure two things: time and distance. The distance an object travels in a period of time tells you its speed. Fast-moving objects go long distances in a short period of time. Slow-moving objects take longer to travel the same distance.

The Explore Activity demonstrates how to measure walking speed and running speed. Your running speed is faster than your walking speed. This means you can run a distance in a shorter amount of time than you can walk it. This chart shows what different speeds mean.

NATIONAL GEOGRAPHIC
FUNtastic Facts

A cheetah can reach speeds up to 60 miles per hour. With its flexible spine and long legs, the cat springs forward like an arrow shot from a bow. Could a cheetah pass cars on a highway?

	SPEED	DISTANCE	TIME	WHAT IT MEANS
Bicycle	24 kilometers per hour	24 kilometers	1 hour	The bicycle travels 24 kilometers in 1 hour.
Swimmer	20 meters per minute	20 meters	1 minute	The swimmer swims 20 meters in 1 minute.
Insect	140 centimeters per second	140 centimeters	1 second	The insect flies 140 centimeters in 1 second.

READING CHARTS
WRITE What is the speed of the swimmer?

What Do Maps Tell You?

A map is a flat drawing that tells you where objects are located. Maps tell you the positions of things.

You could draw a map like the one shown here. Maps tell you how to find things. To read a map, you need to use directions. Maps tell you which direction—north, south, east, or west, to find places or things. These directions help you find your way around.

READING MAPS

1. **WRITE** In which direction would you walk to go from the basketball court to the playground?
2. In which direction is the track from the school?
3. **DISCUSS** How would you go from the front door of the school to the playground without going off the sidewalk?
4. Start at the front door of the school. Walk all the way around the school. Which directions will you go?

WHY IT MATTERS

Motion is everywhere in your world. Your body moves when you run fast and even when you are sitting quietly. You know that you are moving because you change position. Sometimes you change position quickly, like when you throw a ball. Sometimes you change position slowly, like when you turn the pages of a book. Wherever you go and whatever you do, you move!

REVIEW

1. What is motion?
2. Two toy cars are rolling on the floor. The red car is moving faster than the green car. Both cars move for three seconds. Which car will move farther?
3. Use position words and distances to tell how to get from your class to the cafeteria.
4. **COMMUNICATE** Three children all live on the same street. Ann lives west of Peter. Peter lives east of Meg. Meg lives west of Ann. Draw a map of their street.
5. **CRITICAL THINKING Apply** A train is traveling at a speed of 60 miles per hour. How far will it travel after three hours?

WHY IT MATTERS THINK ABOUT IT
Explain how you play your favorite game. Why is it your favorite?

WHY IT MATTERS WRITE ABOUT IT
How are position, motion, and speed important in your favorite game?

NATIONAL GEOGRAPHIC World of SCIENCE

Are We THERE Yet?

Each GPS satellite broadcasts its position with a radio signal. Ships and other vehicles use receivers to pick up the signals.

Science, Technology, and Society

What if you're on a hike in the woods? How can you tell which direction you're going so that you don't get lost?

By day, look for the Sun. It's in the east in the morning and the west in the afternoon. At night, use the Big Dipper to help you find the North Star. Better yet, bring a compass. Its needle always points north.

How do you know how far you've gone? You could count every step. Each step is about two feet. Better yet, wear a pedometer. It's a tool that counts steps. If you know where you started, which direction you're heading, and how far you've gone, you can use a good map to figure out exactly where you are.

Long ago, sailors used stars or a compass to check direction. To check their speed, they tossed a piece of wood into the water. Then they timed how long it took for the ship to move past the wood.

Today there's a new way for travelers to figure out where they are. It's the Global Positioning System (GPS). It has 24 satellites that orbit Earth and constantly broadcast their positions. People who have special receivers can pick up the signals to figure out their own latitude and longitude. Then they can check a map to see exactly where that point is. Someday you may carry a small receiver as you hike and use GPS to find out if you're there yet!

If you know where north is, you can find east, south, and west, too!

Discussion Starter

1. How can knowing which way is north tell you the other directions?

2. Suggest some uses for the GPS besides finding your way on a vacation trip.

interNET CONNECTION To learn more about finding directions, visit www.mhschool.com/science and enter the keyword **LOST.**

Topic 2
PHYSICAL SCIENCE

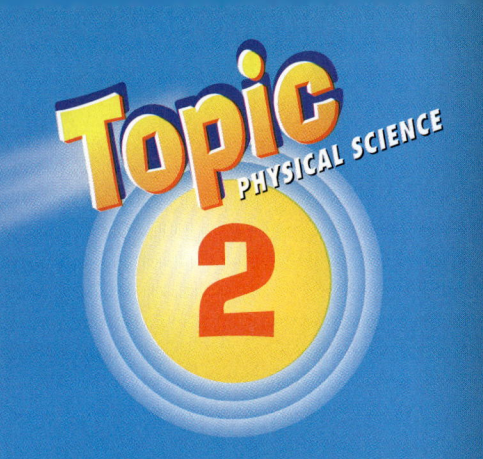

WHY IT MATTERS

You use pushes and pulls in many ways each day.

SCIENCE WORDS

force a push or pull

gravity the pulling force between two objects

weight the pull of gravity on an object

Pushes and Pulls

Why are some things harder to push or pull than others? Every day you use pushes and pulls to get things done. Sometimes you use a big push, like when you push your bike up a hill. Other times you use a small pull, like when you pull open a book.

Which push or pull pictured do you think was easiest? How do you know?

EXPLORE

HYPOTHESIZE Why are some objects harder to push or pull than others? Write a hypothesis in your *Science Journal*. How might you test your ideas?

EXPLORE ACTIVITY

Investigate Why Some Objects Are Harder to Pull

Measure the strength of different pulls.

PROCEDURES

SAFETY: Wear goggles.

MATERIALS
- spring scale
- safety goggles
- 5 objects from your classroom
- Science Journal

1. **OBSERVE** Look at your spring scale. What is the highest your scale can read?

2. **PREDICT** Which one of the objects will require the greatest pull to move? Record your prediction in your *Science Journal*. Then predict which object will require the next strongest pull to move. Record this prediction. Make a prediction for each of your objects.

3. **MEASURE** Hook the scale on an object. Place the scale and the object on a smooth, flat surface and pull at a steady speed. Record what the spring scale reads. Repeat with other classroom objects. Were your predictions correct?

CONCLUDE AND APPLY

1. **IDENTIFY** What did you feel when you pulled an object on the spring scale?

2. **IDENTIFY** Which objects made the scale read the highest when you pulled them?

3. **EXPLAIN** Why did it take a bigger pull to move some objects?

GOING FURTHER: Apply

4. **EXPERIMENT** How could you measure the strength of the pull needed to move your lunch box? If you took your lunch out of your lunch box, how would that affect your measurement?

Why Are Some Objects Harder to Pull?

The Explore Activity shows that a spring scale can be used to measure different pulls. Spring scales measure in *newtons*. A newton is the unit used to measure pushes and pulls. The heavier an object is, the harder you must pull it to get it to move. The harder you pull, the greater the number of newtons the spring scale shows. When you pull an object, you feel a pull, too.

All pulls are **forces** (fôrs′ əz). A force can change the motion of an object. Pushes are forces, too. You see examples of forces in everyday life. You use a pulling force when you put on your backpack. You use a pushing force when you open a door. Do you think you could measure these forces in newtons? Which force would be greater?

FACTS ABOUT FORCES

1 *All pushes and pulls are forces.* Pushes move away from you. Pulls move toward you.

2 *Forces may change the motion of an object.* The heavier an object is, the more force you need to move it.

3 *Forces work in pairs.* Whenever you push or pull on something, you feel a push or pull, too. The push or pull that you feel is a force working in the opposite direction.

4 Even though all forces push or pull, there are *different kinds of forces.* Some forces push and pull on objects without even touching them. One of those forces is acting on you right now. Do you know what it is?

READING DIAGRAMS

1. **WRITE** In which direction do pushes move?
2. **DISCUSS** Do you need more or less force to move a heavier object?

79

What Force Is Always Pulling on You?

There is one force that is everywhere. The force of **gravity** (grav′i tē) is pulling on you right now. Gravity is the pulling force between two objects. It attracts, or pulls, objects together. It pulls everything on Earth.

The force of gravity between two objects depends on two things. It depends on how much *matter* is in the objects and how close they are to each other. Matter is what makes up an object. The more matter there is in the objects, and the closer the objects are to each other, the stronger the force of gravity between them will be.

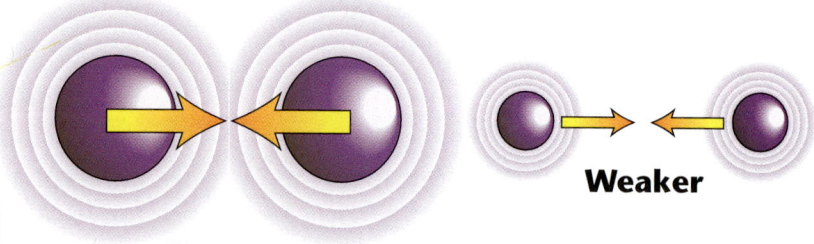

Stronger   **Weaker**

When things go up, the force of gravity pulls them down. Things fall to Earth because they are pulled by Earth's gravity. Most objects don't have enough matter in them to pull on each other enough to notice. Earth has a lot of matter. The pull between it and other objects is strong.

Brain Power

How would a basketball game change if there were no gravity? Draw a picture or write a story that shows what the game would be like.

Why Are Some Things Heavier than Others?

Some objects are heavy. Other objects are light. You can measure how heavy or light something is by measuring its **weight** (wāt). Weight is the pull of gravity on an object. Why do some things weigh more than others? Objects that weigh more have more matter in them. The more matter there is in an object, the greater the pull of gravity is on that object.

Scientists measure weight in newtons. In everyday life, people in the United States measure weight in *pounds*. A pound is the unit used to measure forces (such as weight) in the English system of measurement. Newtons are the unit of force in the metric system. All scientists use the metric system.

The pull of gravity is just about the same all over Earth. So the weight of an object will be about the same anywhere on Earth. However, the pull of gravity is different on other planets. So objects might weigh more or less on different planets.

These apples weigh two pounds or nine newtons.

SKILL BUILDER

Skill: Interpreting Data

READING A BAR GRAPH

The bar graph below shows how much the dog weighs on each planet and on the Moon. Each bar gives us information, or *data*. For example, look at the bar labeled Earth. It lines up with 40 on the Pounds scale on the left. Now look at the bar labeled Jupiter. What number on the Pounds scale does it line up with? By answering this question, you are interpreting data.

Interpret the data in this graph to answer the questions below.

MATERIALS
- *Science Journal*

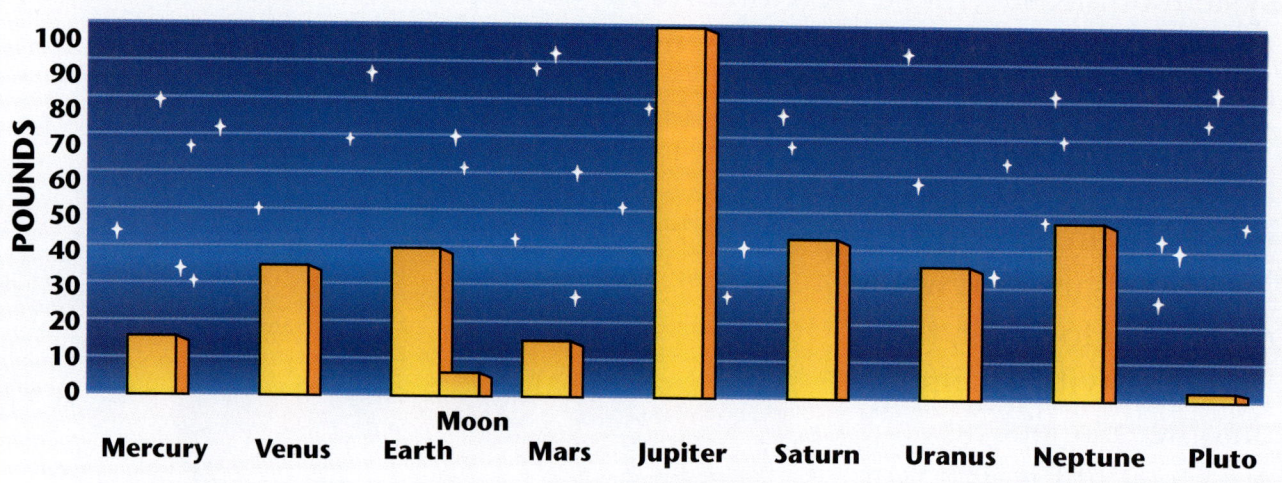

PROCEDURES

1. **INTERPRET DATA** How much does the dog weigh on Mars?

2. **INTERPRET DATA** On which planets would the dog weigh more than on Earth? On which planets would the dog weigh less?

3. **COMPARE** How much heavier is the dog on Jupiter than on Venus?

This dog weighs 40 pounds on Earth. How much does it weigh on other planets?

CONCLUDE AND APPLY

COMMUNICATE Make a chart showing how you interpreted the data from the graph in question 2.

82

Why Does a Dog Weigh Less on Mars?

Remember that the more matter an object has, the greater the pull of gravity. Jupiter has more matter than Earth, so the force of gravity is greater there. The stronger pull of gravity makes things weigh more on Jupiter.

On the other hand, Mars has less matter than Earth. The pull of gravity is weaker there. The weaker pull of gravity makes things weigh less on Mars.

WHY IT MATTERS

Almost everything you do requires a force of some type. When you brush your hair, you push your hair back. When you write your name, you push and pull the pencil across the paper. As you push and pull on things around you, one force is always pulling on you. Gravity is pulling on you and everything else on Earth all the time.

REVIEW

1. What is a force?
2. How do you use pushes and pulls in your everyday life?
3. If you took your books out of your backpack, how would that change the amount of force needed to lift the backpack?
4. **INTERPRET DATA** Look back at the graph on page 82. How much does the dog weigh on Uranus?
5. **CRITICAL THINKING** *Apply* A planet has six times as much matter as Earth. Do you think an object would weigh more on this planet or less? Explain.

WHY IT MATTERS THINK ABOUT IT
A hairbrush is a tool that you use to make your hair smoother. A pencil is a tool you use for writing. Describe three other tools you use each day.

WHY IT MATTERS WRITE ABOUT IT
Knives, forks, and spoons are tools you use for eating. How do pushes and pulls help you use these tools?

SCIENCE MAGAZINE

SHOW YOUR MUSCLES

Let's hear it for your muscles! They're what help you move and stay on the go. They help you run to score that touchdown, climb trees, swim and dive, and so much more!

When you push or pull, you use muscles. Some of them come in pairs. Your upper arm has biceps and triceps. Both muscles stretch between a bone in your upper arm and one in your lower arm.

How are these children using their muscles?

Health Link

Muscles contract, or get shorter. When your biceps contracts, it pulls on the lower bone. Your lower arm moves up so you can lift objects. How would you carry all your books without biceps?

You use your triceps to push things. When your triceps contracts, your biceps relaxes. Your arm becomes straighter and you can push down.

Want to run a little faster? Hit a ball a little harder? The more you push and pull, the stronger your muscles get.

Walking, jogging, and swimming build up muscles in your whole body. They make many muscles pull against gravity.

Here's how to use gravity to strengthen your muscles:

- ✓ Increase the amount of weight you pull or push.
- ✓ Increase the amount of time you push or pull that weight.
- ✓ Increase how often you push or pull that weight.

Remember that muscles need time to rest between exercise sessions!

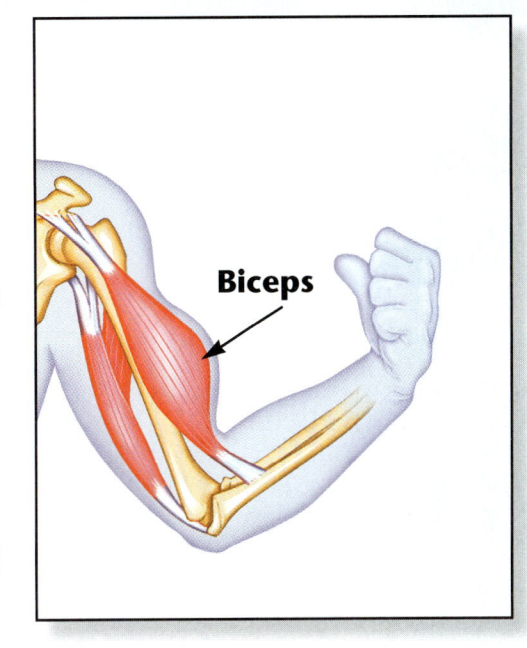

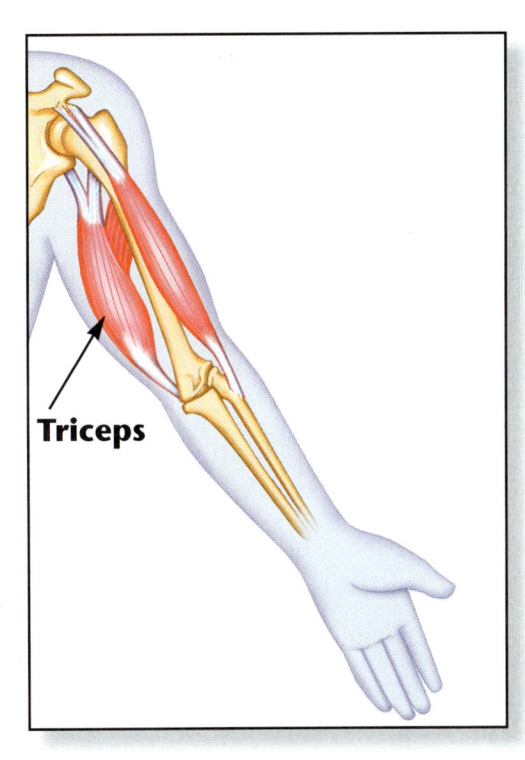

DISCUSSION STARTER

1. What kinds of things do you do that use your biceps and triceps?
2. What activities do you enjoy that use your whole body?

To learn more about your muscles, visit *www.mhschool.com/science* and enter the keyword MUSCLES.

*inter*NET CONNECTION

Topic 3
PHYSICAL SCIENCE

WHY IT MATTERS

Forces can change an object's motion.

SCIENCE WORDS

friction a force that occurs when one object rubs against another

Forces in Motion

What must these children do in order to make their seesaw move? Just a few minutes ago, the seesaw was bobbing up and down. Then it stopped. What do you think caused it to stop? Why did it stop in the position it's in?

EXPLORE

HYPOTHESIZE Sometimes objects change position, and sometimes they stay still. What must you do to make a resting object move? Write a hypothesis in your *Science Journal*. How might you test your ideas?

EXPLORE ACTIVITY

Investigate What Causes a Change in Motion

Experiment to find out what makes a resting object move.

PROCEDURES

SAFETY: Wear goggles.

1. Cut two pieces of string that are slightly shorter than the width of your desk. Knot the strings together. Lay the knot in the middle of your desk and let the strings hang off opposite sides of the desk. Bend the paper clips to make hooks, and tie one to the free end of each string.

2. **PREDICT** Hold the knot in place and hang two washers on one paper-clip hook. What will happen if you let go of the knot? Write your prediction in your *Science Journal*. Test your prediction.

3. **PREDICT** Take the two washers off. Holding the knot in place, add one washer to each of the paper-clip hooks. Predict what will happen if you let go of the knot now. Test your prediction.

4. **EXPERIMENT** What could you do with the washers to move the knot toward one side of the desk? Test your idea.

MATERIALS
- washers
- 2 paper clips
- scissors
- string
- safety goggles
- *Science Journal*

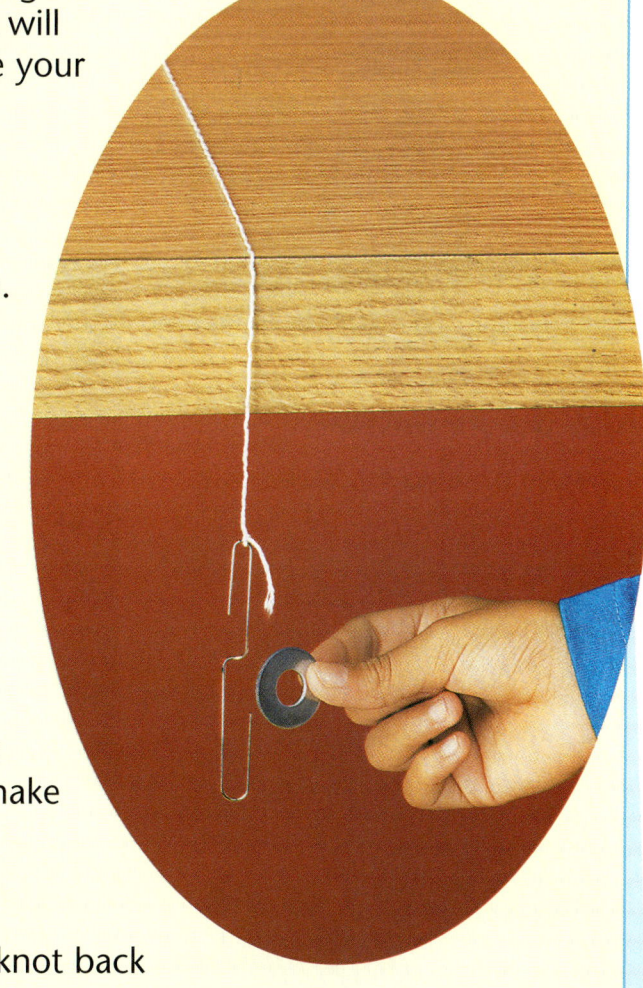

CONCLUDE AND APPLY

1. **COMPARE** What did you observe in steps 2 and 3?

2. **EXPLAIN** In step 3, why didn't the knot move? In step 4, what did you do to make the knot move?

GOING FURTHER: Problem Solving

3. **EXPERIMENT** How could you move the knot back to the middle of your desk?

87

What Is a Change in Motion?

The Explore Activity shows that when there is one washer at each end of a piece of string, the knot in the center of the string does not move. However, when different amounts of weights are placed on the string, the knot moves.

When an object that is resting starts to move, there is a change in motion. A change in motion also occurs when a moving object speeds up, slows down, changes direction, or stops.

Here are the different types of changes in motion.

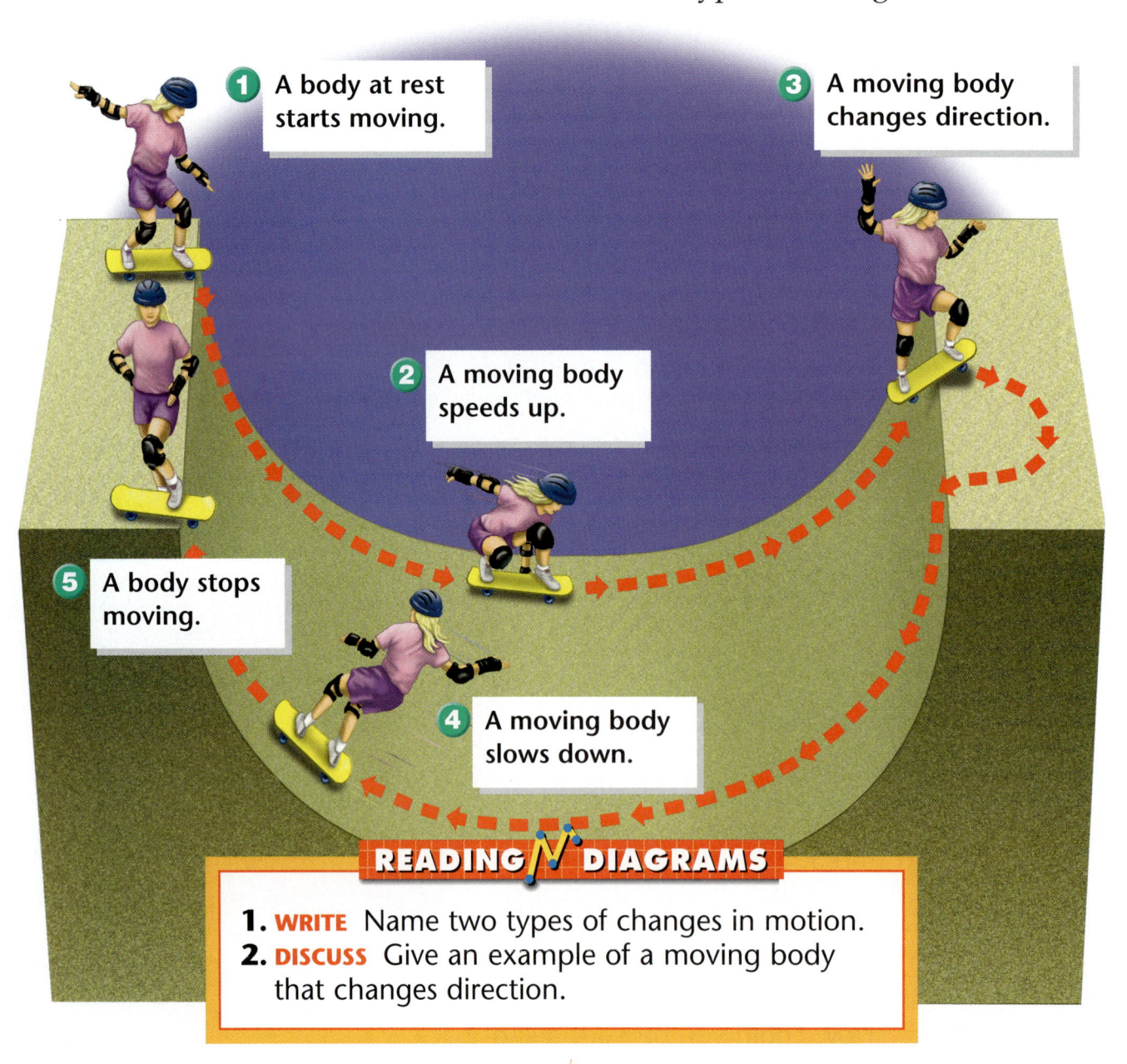

1. A body at rest starts moving.
2. A moving body speeds up.
3. A moving body changes direction.
4. A moving body slows down.
5. A body stops moving.

READING DIAGRAMS

1. **WRITE** Name two types of changes in motion.
2. **DISCUSS** Give an example of a moving body that changes direction.

What Causes a Change in Motion?

In the Explore Activity, one washer was put on each string. Two forces were acting on the knot at one time. The forces were balanced, so there was no change in motion. The knot stayed at rest. When different amounts of weights were put on the strings, the forces didn't balance anymore. There was a change in motion—the knot moved.

A change in an object's motion is the result of all the forces that are acting on the object. The same thing happens on a seesaw. You see a change in motion only when forces are unbalanced. Think of what happens when you get off a seesaw. The forces suddenly become unbalanced. Then the seesaw moves.

You can see how unbalanced forces create a change in motion in a tug-of-war. When both sides pull equally, forces balance. Nothing moves.

If one side begins to pull harder, the forces become unbalanced. Now there is a change in the position of the rope.

equal forces: no motion

unequal forces: motion

What happens if the rope breaks?

Robert Shurney, with glasses, is an inventor. He designed the tires that were used on the buggy driven by astronauts on the Moon.

Why Do Things Stop Moving?

A ball is rolling on the floor. Over time, it slows down. A force must be acting on the ball.

The force that slows the ball down is called **friction** (frik' shən). Friction is a force that occurs when one object rubs against another. The ball rubbing on the floor creates friction.

Different materials produce different amounts of friction. Rough materials rub best. They produce a lot of friction. Most smooth materials don't rub well. They produce less friction. Other materials, like rubber, are smooth but still produce a lot of friction.

Friction keeps the car's rubber tires on the road, but ice on the road changes the amount of friction. The car slides!

Brain Power
Sand is sometimes put on icy roads. How does sand change the amount of friction on an icy road?

What objects rub together when you ride a bike? Friction slows the bike down even if you are riding on a very smooth sidewalk. You have to keep pedaling in order to keep the bike in motion.

How do brakes stop a bike's motion? When you squeeze the brake lever, the brake pad presses against the wheel. There is friction between the brake pad and the rim of the wheel. The wheel slows down. The bike stops.

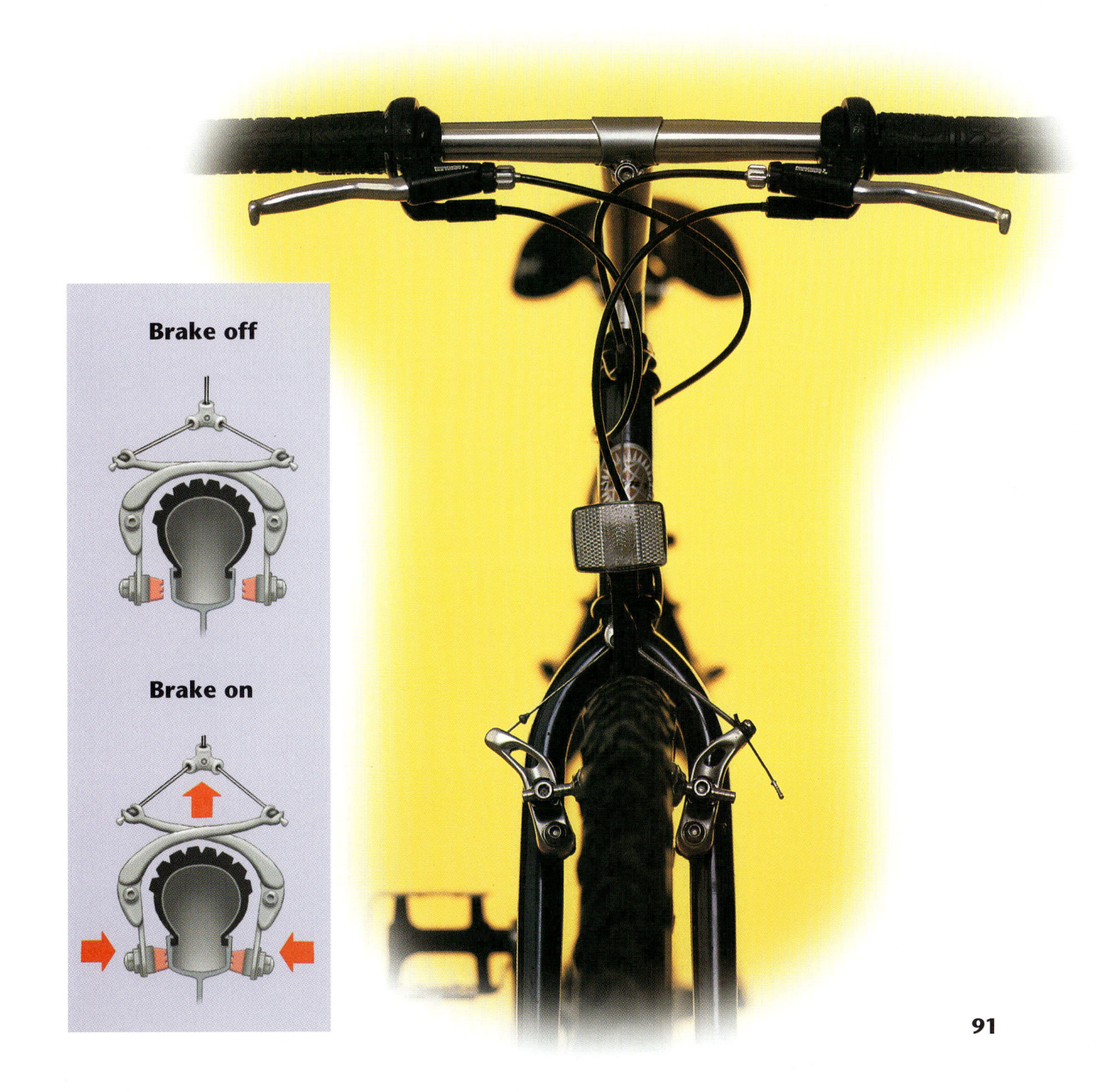

Brake off

Brake on

How Can You Control Friction?

Friction is a force that slows things down. You can't get rid of friction, but you can change the amount of friction you have. People use slippery things to decrease friction. For example, oil is often put on the moving parts of machines. To increase friction, people use rough or sticky things. In-line skates have a rubber pad that skaters use to slow down and stop.

QUICK LAB

Marbles in Motion

HYPOTHESIZE How can marbles help you reduce friction? Write a hypothesis in your *Science Journal*.

PROCEDURES

1. **OBSERVE** Push the wooden block over the surface of your desk. Describe how it feels in your *Science Journal*.

2. **EXPERIMENT** Place the marbles under the jar lid. Lay the block on top of the lid.

3. **OBSERVE** Push the block over the surface of your desk again. How does it feel now?

MATERIALS
- 10–20 marbles
- jar lid
- wooden block
- *Science Journal*

CONCLUDE AND APPLY

1. **IDENTIFY** When did you feel more friction: When you pushed the block by itself or over the jar lid?

2. **EXPLAIN** How did the marbles help to reduce friction?

WHY IT MATTERS

Every time you move an object, you are unbalancing the forces acting on it. One force that affects you every day is friction. Without friction, you couldn't grip a door knob, or pick up a ball. You'd slip when you tried to walk. Once you were moving, you wouldn't be able to stop!

How do you make sure you don't slip on the basketball court? Put on some rubber-soled sneakers to increase friction.

REVIEW

1. What is a change in motion?
2. You see a ball resting on the ground. What can you do to make it move?
3. What is friction?
4. **PREDICT** Would it be easier to roller skate on gravel or concrete? How do you know?
5. **CRITICAL THINKING** *Apply* You are swinging on a swing. What must you do to swing higher? What must you do to stop?

WHY IT MATTERS THINK ABOUT IT
Describe some of the sports you like to watch or play. What type of equipment do the players use? What sort of clothing do they wear?

WHY IT MATTERS WRITE ABOUT IT
How does the clothing or equipment used in your favorite sport help the players to control friction?

READING SKILL Look at the diagram of the tug-of-war on page 89. Write a paragraph that explains what the diagram shows.

SCIENCE MAGAZINE

DANCING ON ROCKS

A Closer Look

Special Tools

All this equipment is needed for safe climbing.

What's dancing got to do with rocks? Ask someone whose favorite sport is rock climbing. A climber will tell you it's like dancing on the side of a cliff. Like a dancer, a rock climber has to understand the use of friction and balance.

Climbers need friction as they climb. Their shoes have sticky rubber soles to keep their feet from slipping on the rocks. Climbers carry bags of chalk on their belts. As they climb, they rub chalk on their hands. That helps with the friction between their hands and the rocks.

Rock climbers use ropes as they climb, but not to pull themselves up. The ropes are for safety. They hang on the special harness climbers wear.

As climbers move, they put special metal bolts into cracks in the rock. Then they clip their ropes to each bolt. If a climber slips, the last bolt will grip the rope tightly. Friction will stop the rope from slipping. Climbers may fall a short way, but their ropes will stop them from falling too far. Then they can start climbing again.

Rock climbers learn to balance gracefully, like dancers. They know it's important to keep their weight evenly on both feet. If they lean, they lose their balance. Then they could really fall!

DISCUSSION STARTERS

1. What equipment helps rock climbers use friction?
2. How do rock climbers keep their balance while climbing?

To learn more about rock climbing, visit www.mhschool.com/science and enter the keyword CLIMBERS.

*inter*NET CONNECTION

CHAPTER 3 REVIEW

SCIENCE WORDS

force p.78
friction p.90
gravity p.80
motion p.70
position p.68
speed p.71
weight p.81

USING SCIENCE WORDS

Number a paper from 1 to 10. Fill in 1 to 5 with words from the list above

1. An object's location is its ___?___.

2. How fast an object moves is its ___?___.

3. When you throw a ball in the air, it falls down because of ___?___.

4. Snow and ice make the ground have less ___?___.

5. Unbalanced forces cause ___?___.

6–10. Pick five words from the list above. Include all words that were not used in 1 to 5. Write each word in a sentence.

UNDERSTANDING SCIENCE IDEAS

11. How can you measure your speed on a long car trip?

12. Two objects are pushed with the same force. The first object moves twice as far as the second object. Which object is heavier?

USING IDEAS AND SKILLS

13. **READING SKILL: READ A DIAGRAM** How do brakes stop a bike's motion? Hint: Use the diagram on page 91 to help you.

14. **INTERPRET DATA** Who is the fastest runner? What is the speed of the slowest runner?

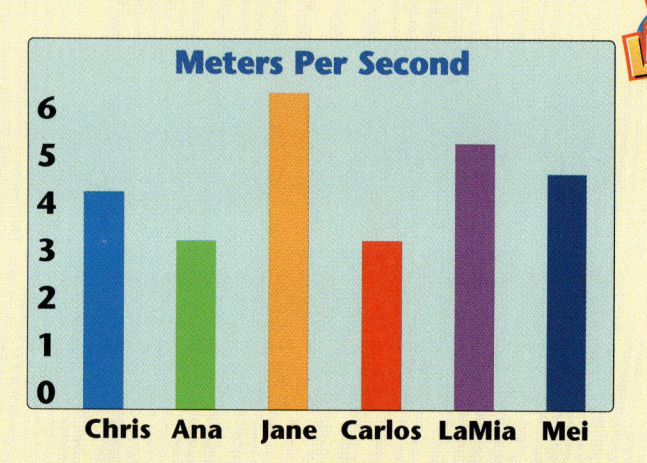

Meters Per Second (bar graph showing: Chris 4, Ana 3, Jane 6, Carlos 3, LaMia 5, Mei 4)

MATH LINK

15. **THINKING LIKE A SCIENTIST** Do dogs or cats run faster? How can you test your ideas?

PROBLEMS and PUZZLES

Long Distance You want to race your friend, who lives in a different country. How could you find out who is faster?

96

CHAPTER 4
WORK AND MACHINES

People do different kinds of work. Machines do work too. How do we define what work is? When is play really work? Read on to find out!

In Chapter 4 you will find some lists. A list gives you facts about something.

Topic 4
PHYSICAL SCIENCE

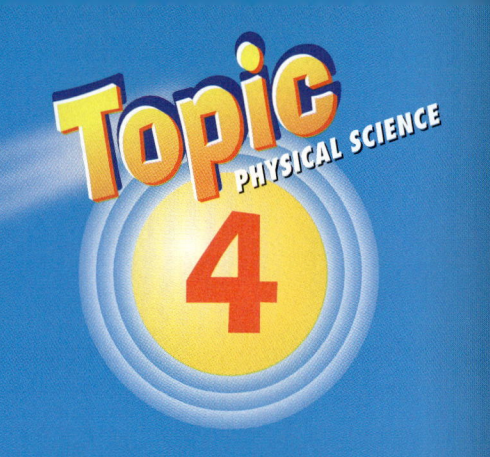

WHY IT MATTERS

Every day you do work. Sometimes play is work, too.

SCIENCE WORDS

work when a force changes the motion of an object

energy the ability to do work

Doing Work

Are you working right now? All day long you do different kinds of work. You do schoolwork at school and homework at home. You may have chores that you do to help your family, too.

Who is doing work in these pictures? How do you know?

EXPLORE

HYPOTHESIZE What do you think work is? In your own words, write a definition of work in your *Science Journal*. How might you apply your definition of work to different kinds of actions?

EXPLORE ACTIVITY

Investigate What Work Is

Use your definition of work to classify the actions below. Does your definition of work make sense?

MATERIALS
- 4 books
- pencil
- *Science Journal*

PROCEDURES

1. **EXPERIMENT** Complete each of the actions described below.

- Put four books on the floor. Lift one book up.
- Put four books on the floor. Lift all four up.
- Put a book on your desk. Push down very hard on top of the book.
- Pick up a pencil from your desk.
- Push against a wall with all of your strength.

2. **CLASSIFY** After each action, ask yourself: "Did I do work?" Review the definition of work that you wrote in your *Science Journal*. Does the action you did fit your definition? Tell your partner what you think. Together, decide whether the action was work or not.

CONCLUDE AND APPLY

1. **EVALUATE** Look at your responses to the question "Did I do work?" Think about your responses. Is there a pattern? What is it?

2. **COMMUNICATE** Write a sentence for each action explaining why you classified it the way you did.

GOING FURTHER: Apply

3. **EVALUATE** How might different people classify the actions? For example, would picking up one book be work for a baby? Would picking up four books be work for a very strong adult?

Is It Work?

The Explore Activity shows several actions. Some of the actions were **work**. Others were not work. You wrote your own definition of work. Is your definition correct? Scientists say that work is done when a force changes the motion of an object.

Take another look at some of the actions shown on pages 98 and 99. Did they involve work or not?

Who's Doing Work?

1. Picking up books
Force: Pulling force of hands
Object: Books
Movement: Books move up.
Conclusion: Work was done because a force changed the motion of the books.
☑ Work
☐ Not Work

2. Pushing against wall
Force: Pushing force of body
Object: Wall
Movement: None
Conclusion: No work was done because there was no change in motion.
☐ Work
☑ Not Work

3. Shaking rattle
Force: Shaking force of arm
Object: Rattle
Movement: Rattle moves back and forth.
Conclusion: Work was done because a force changed the motion of the rattle.
☑ Work
☐ Not Work

Brain Power

A ball is rolling on a flat surface. Is any work being done? You can ignore the effects of friction on the ball. Hint: Is there any change in motion for a ball traveling at a steady speed?

What Do You Need to Get Work Done?

To do work, you need **energy** (en′ ər jē). Energy is the ability to do work.

Energy exists in different forms. Moving things, like a rock rolling down a hill, have energy of motion. Sometimes objects have the ability to move because of their position. A rock that is on top of a hill is in a position to move. Energy that can cause an object to move is called stored energy. Sources of stored energy include food, fuel, and batteries.

Other forms of energy include heat, light, sound, and electricity.

A rock rolling down a hill has energy. How might a falling rock do work?

Quick Lab

Changing Energy

HYPOTHESIZE What will happen when you rub a wooden block with sandpaper? Write a hypothesis in your *Science Journal*.

MATERIALS
- wooden block
- sandpaper
- safety goggles
- *Science Journal*

PROCEDURES

SAFETY: Wear goggles.

1. **OBSERVE** Feel the temperature of the block.

2. **OBSERVE** Rub the block with sandpaper about 20 times. What do you feel through your fingertips?

CONCLUDE AND APPLY

EXPLAIN What happened to the temperature of the block?

How Does Energy Change?

Energy moves from place to place, and changes from one form to another. The Quick Lab shows how friction can change to heat. The steps below show how energy of motion can move from one object to another.

READING DIAGRAMS

1. **WRITE** How many changes of motion did you see in the diagram? Make a list.
2. **DISCUSS** Why did the green ball stop moving after hitting the yellow ball?

1 The green ball has energy of motion.

2 The green ball hits the yellow ball. Now the yellow ball has energy of motion. The force of the green ball has caused the yellow ball's motion to change.

3 Work has been done on the yellow ball. It has gained energy from the green ball.

4 The green ball has stopped moving. Its energy of motion went to the yellow ball.

102

WHY IT MATTERS

When people talk about work, they usually mean a job that adults do. Whether you have a job or not, you work every day. You work when you pedal a bike. You work when you jump rope. You even work a little bit when you do your homework! Where do you get the energy to do all this work? From the energy stored in food! Food is the fuel your body uses to do the work you do each day.

REVIEW

1. You push against a brick wall as hard as you can. Your friend picks up a pencil. Who did more work?
2. What is energy?
3. How does energy change?
4. **INFER** Rub your hands together quickly. What energy change takes place?
5. **CRITICAL THINKING** *Apply* Write a definition of work. How did your definition change after finishing this lesson?

WHY IT MATTERS THINK ABOUT IT
Describe a job you would like to have when you grow up. Why do you think you would like it?

WHY IT MATTERS WRITE ABOUT IT
What kinds of actions would you do in the job you would like to have? Would you be doing a lot of work the way a scientist would define it?

SCIENCE MAGAZINE

Earth at Work

What kind of work does Earth do? It's not the same kind of work you do when you clean your room. Oh, no. Earth works a lot harder than that! Earth uses lots more energy to put rocks and soil in motion.

Deep within Earth there are layers of rock. These rock layers push against each other without moving. Energy builds up or is stored up between the layers.

Earth Science Link

Earthquakes can cause great damage.

An earthquake can release stored energy in rocks and cause a landslide.

Sometimes the rubbing and pushing breaks the rocks. Or the rubbing and pushing can make rock layers slide or pop out of place. The energy that builds up in the rocks is suddenly released. It's an earthquake!

Deep down beneath the surface of Earth, there are melted rocks. They are very, very hot. Sometimes an earthquake cracks a hard rock layer around the melted rock. It pushes up through the cracks to Earth's surface. The melted rock blasts or flows from the ground as lava.

Some of the lava's heat energy becomes mechanical, or moving, energy. Rivers of lava push everything out of their way. When the lava cools, it forms a volcano.

Rocks and soil on hills can become loose during an earthquake. This makes the solid rock under the surface of the hill weaker. The loose rocks and soil on the hill begin to fall. It's a landslide!

DISCUSSION STARTER

1. How can an earthquake help to form a volcano?
2. Do you think we'll ever be able to use the energy from volcanoes, earthquakes, or landslides? Why or why not?

To learn more about Earth's forces, visit www.mhschool.com/science and enter the keyword QUAKES.

interNET CONNECTION

Topic 5
PHYSICAL SCIENCE

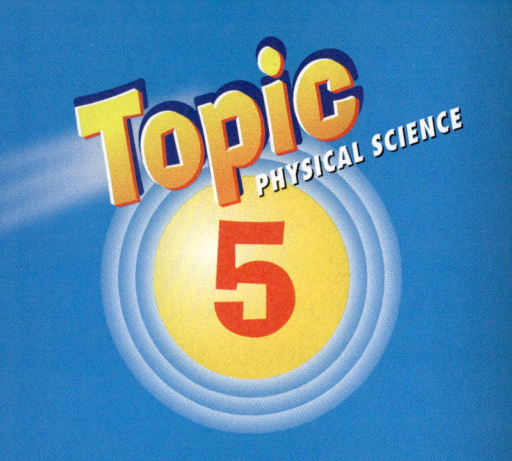

WHY IT MATTERS

Tools can help you get work done faster and easier.

SCIENCE WORDS

machine a tool that makes work easier to do

simple machine a machine with few or no moving parts

lever a straight bar that moves on a fixed point

wheel and axle a wheel that turns on a post

pulley a simple machine that uses a wheel and a rope

Getting Work Done

Can you help these children with their gardening? They want to start planting, but there is a big rock right in the middle of the garden! They try pushing. They try pulling. No matter what they do, the rock is too heavy to move. What would you do? Can you think of a plan that would help you move the heavy rock?

EXPLORE

HYPOTHESIZE Sometimes you want to move an object that takes a lot of force to move. How can you do it? Write a hypothesis in your *Science Journal*. How might you test your ideas?

EXPLORE ACTIVITY

Design Your Own Experiment

HOW CAN YOU MAKE WORK EASIER?

PROCEDURES

SAFETY: Wear goggles.

1. **ASK QUESTIONS** How can you invent a way to get the roll of tape from the floor to your desk? Your hands can help provide the lift, but you can't just pick up the tape and put it on the desk.

2. **COMMUNICATE** With your group members, think of as many different ways as you can to lift the tape. Write or draw two of your plans in your *Science Journal*.

3. **EXPERIMENT** After your teacher approves your plans, try one of them. Write down what happens. Does the plan work well? If not, what can you do to fix it? Try your other plan for lifting the tape.

MATERIALS
- a roll of masking tape
- safety goggles
- building materials
- *Science Journal*

CONCLUDE AND APPLY

1. **COMPARE AND CONTRAST** Which of your two plans worked better?

2. **IDENTIFY** What materials did you use in your most successful invention?

3. **EXPLAIN** What forces did you use? What force did you work against?

GOING FURTHER: Apply

4. **EVALUATE** Why did you think some plans for lifting the tape worked better than others?

How Can You Make Work Easier?

You need to move something. Normally, you move things with your hands. The Explore Activity demonstrates that sometimes you might need to find another way to get a job done. You may need a **machine** (mə shēn′).

What is a machine? A machine is a tool that makes work easier to do. From Lesson 4, you remember that work is done when a force changes the motion of an object. How do machines make it easier for forces to move objects?

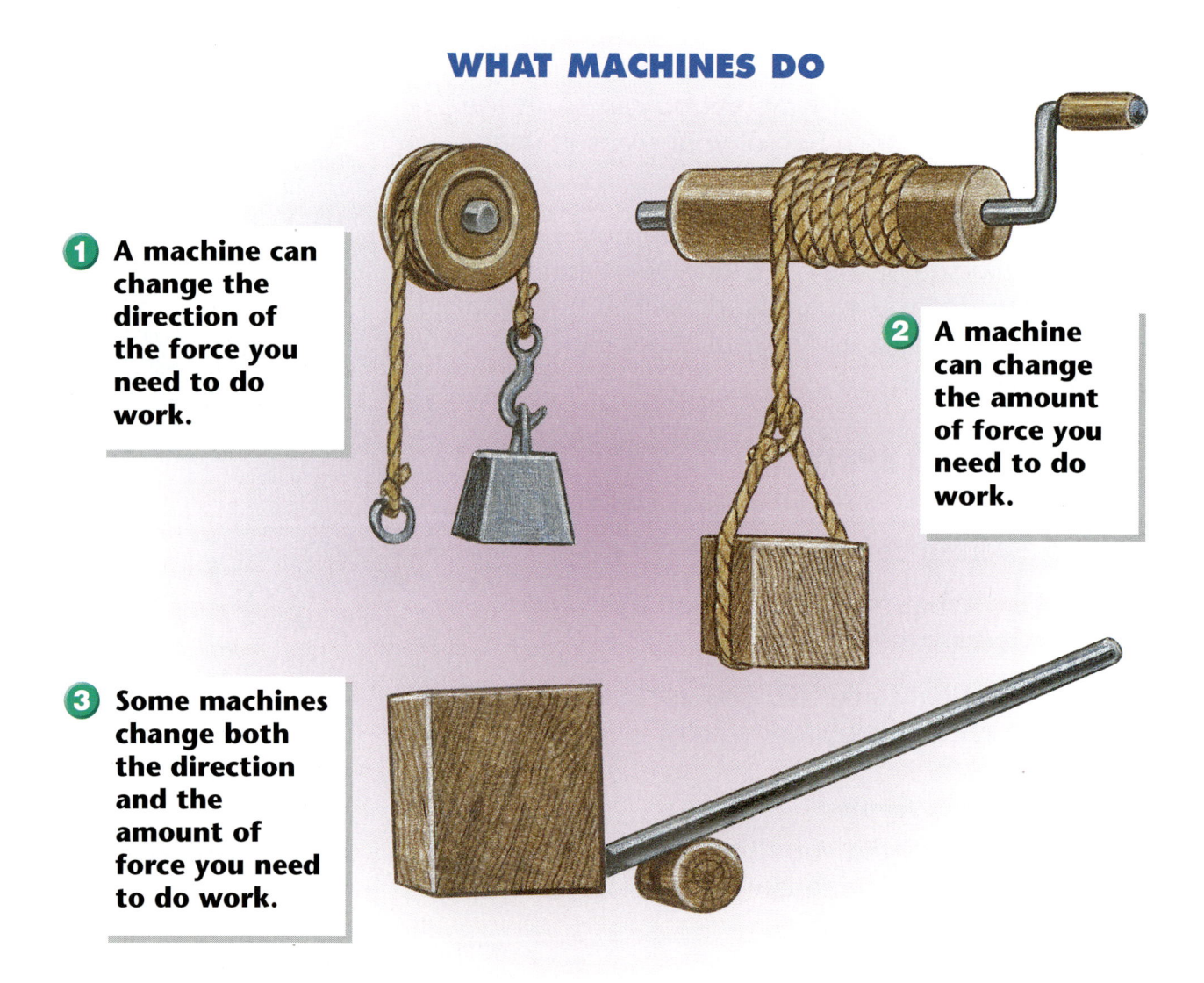

WHAT MACHINES DO

1. A machine can change the direction of the force you need to do work.

2. A machine can change the amount of force you need to do work.

3. Some machines change both the direction and the amount of force you need to do work.

What Is a Simple Machine?

A **simple machine** (sim′ pəl mə shēn′) is often used to make work easier. Machines with few or no moving parts are called simple machines. A **lever** (lev′ ər) is an example of a simple machine. A lever is a straight bar that moves on a fixed point. All levers have three important parts: the load, the fulcrum, and the force.

HOW LEVERS MAKE WORK EASIER

A lever makes moving a load easier in two ways. A lever lets you change the direction of a force. Sometimes it is easier to push one way than another. A lever lets you change the amount of force needed to move something.

The force is the push or pull that moves the lever.

The load is the object being lifted or moved.

The fulcrum is the point where the lever turns.

READING DIAGRAMS

1. **DISCUSS** How do levers make work easier?
2. **REPRESENT** Draw a lever. Label the force, load, and fulcrum.

109

load
force
fulcrum

The load is in the middle on a wheelbarrow.

Are There Different Kinds of Levers?

The world is full of levers. Each one is set up differently. The force, fulcrum, and load can change places. Sometimes the fulcrum is in the middle. Sometimes it is on the outside. Take a look at how this lever works.

QUICK LAB

Make a Lever

HYPOTHESIZE What happens when you change the position of the fulcrum on a lever? Write a hypothesis in your *Science Journal*.

PROCEDURES

1. Use some clay to hold a pencil in place on your desk. Place the ruler over the center of the pencil.

2. **EXPERIMENT** Put 2 blocks on one end of your ruler. Add pieces of clay to the other end of the ruler. How much clay does it take to lift the blocks? What happens if you take a block away?

3. **EXPERIMENT** Change the position of the ruler on the pencil. Then repeat step 2. How does the new position change your results?

MATERIALS
- clay
- ruler
- pencil
- 2 small blocks
- *Science Journal*

CONCLUDE AND APPLY

1. **COMMUNICATE** Draw your lever. Label the force, load, and fulcrum. Describe how your lever works.

2. **DRAW CONCLUSIONS** How does the position of the pencil affect the amount of force you need to lift the load?

What Are Some Other Simple Machines?

Another kind of simple machine is the **wheel and axle** (hwēl and ak′sel). This simple machine has a wheel that turns on a post. The post is called an axle.

A wheel and axle makes work easier by changing the strength of a turning force. The wheel turns a long distance. The axle turns a short distance.

This windlass is used to raise water from a well. The bucket is tied to a rope. The other end of the rope is tied to the axle. At the end of the axle is the handle. When you turn the handle in a large circle, the axle turns in a small circle. The bucket moves up.

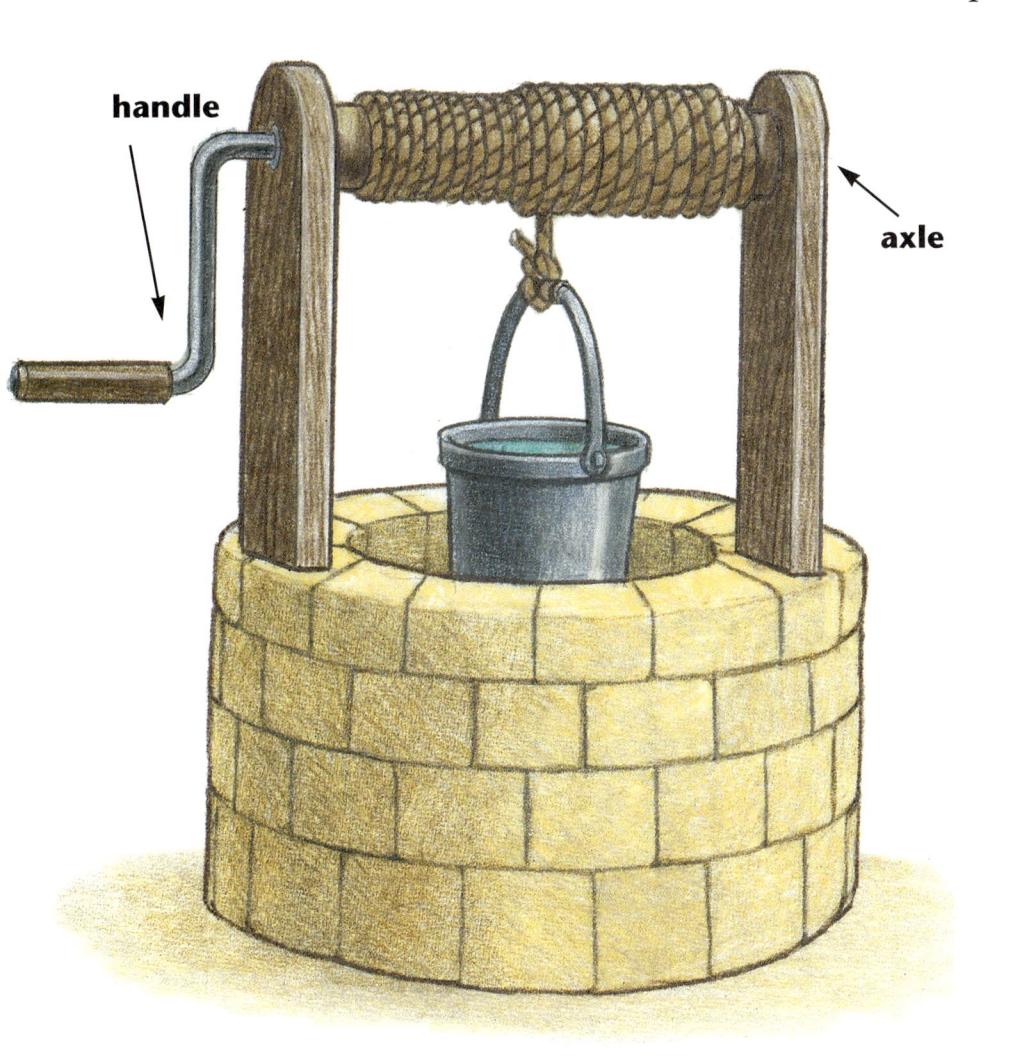

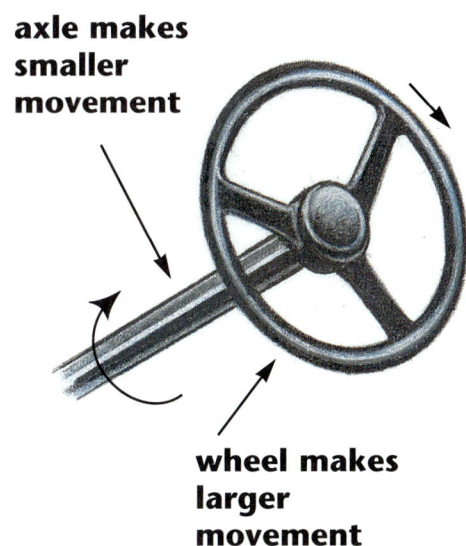

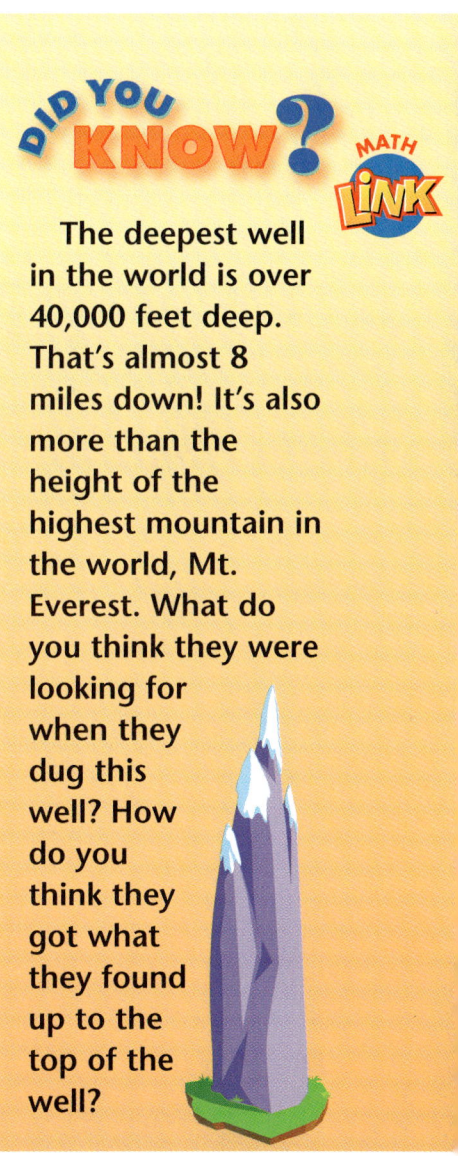

axle makes smaller movement

wheel makes larger movement

handle

axle

DID YOU KNOW? MATH LINK

The deepest well in the world is over 40,000 feet deep. That's almost 8 miles down! It's also more than the height of the highest mountain in the world, Mt. Everest. What do you think they were looking for when they dug this well? How do you think they got what they found up to the top of the well?

111

What Goes Down to Go Up?

Another simple machine is the **pulley** (pul′ē). A pulley is a simple machine that uses a wheel and a rope to lift a load. Some pulleys make work easier simply by changing the direction of a force. In a one-wheel pulley, the force and the load are equal. The pulley lets you pull down to lift the load up.

Some pulleys make work easier by changing the amount of force needed to do the work. A two-wheel pulley makes the job easier by reducing the amount of force needed to move the load.

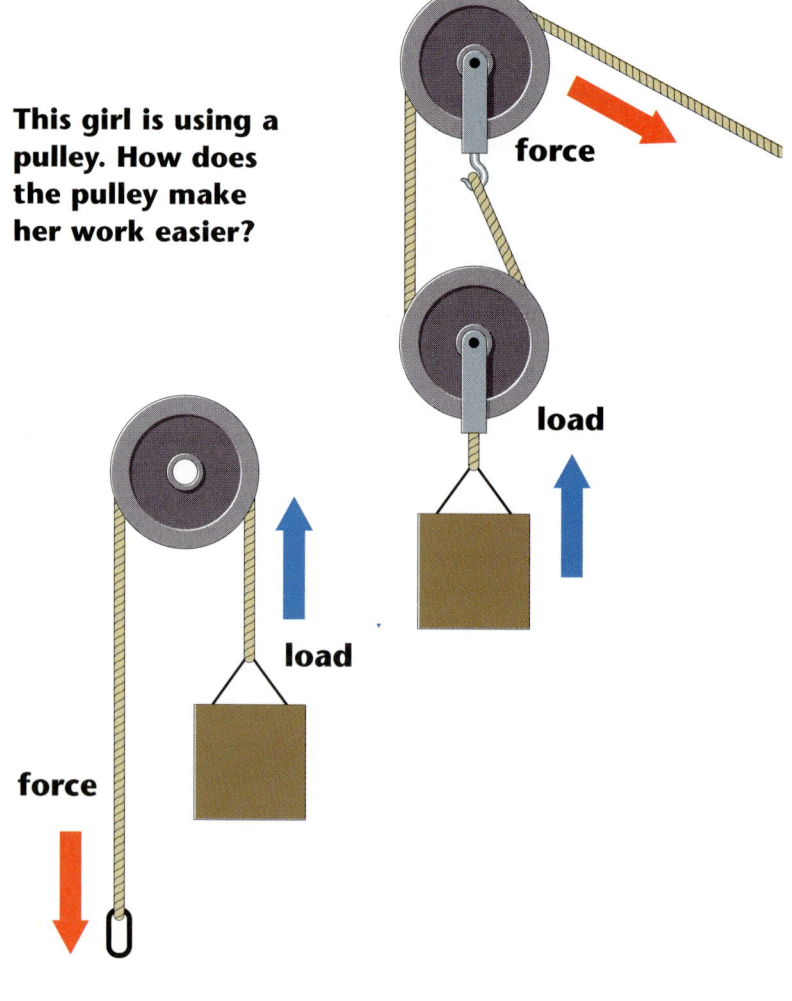

This girl is using a pulley. How does the pulley make her work easier?

A pulley is actually a lever. So is a wheel and axle. Look at the diagrams. The same object is being lifted in each picture, but a different simple machine is doing the work.

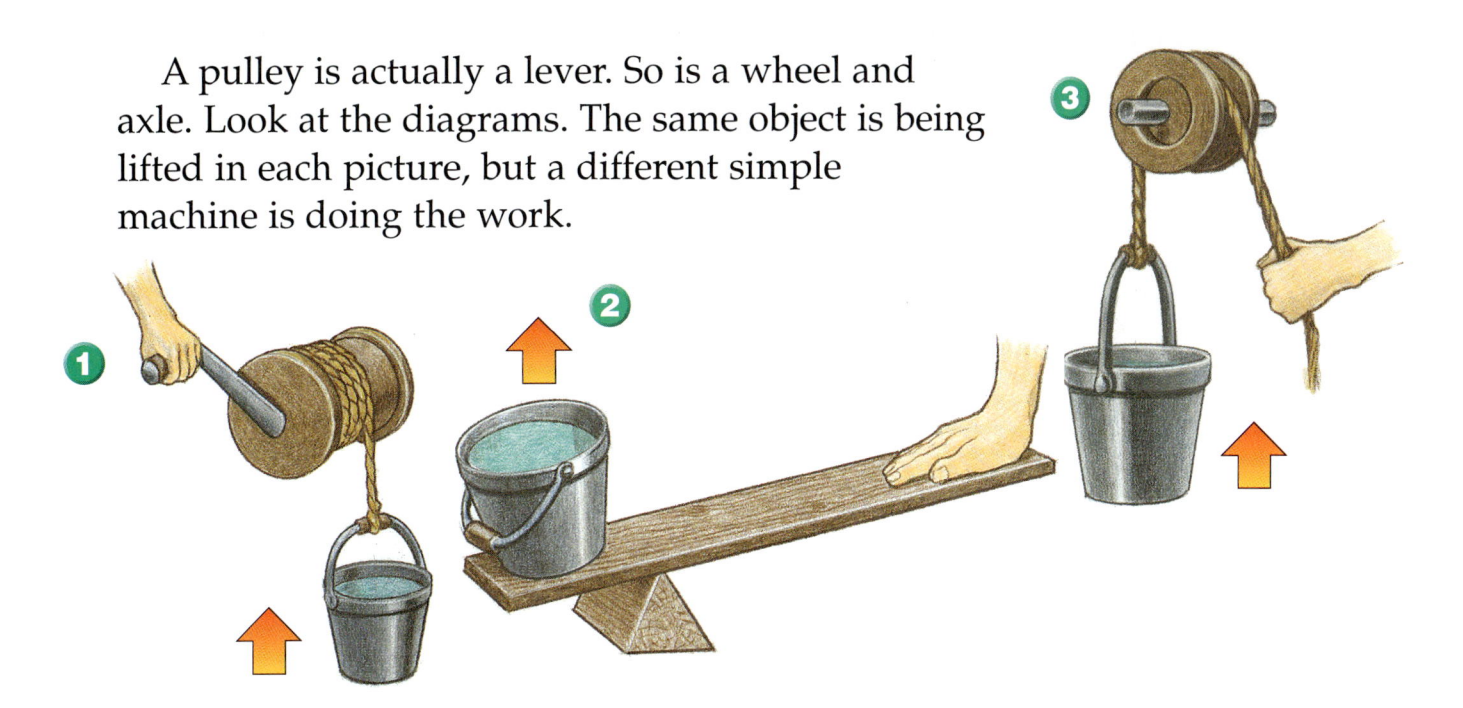

WHY IT MATTERS

You are surrounded by machines. If you don't believe it, take a look around. A spoon is a type of lever, and so is a bottle opener. Even your arms, legs, and fingers are levers!

REVIEW

1. How do machines make work easier?

2. What is a simple machine?

3. What kind of simple machine will help you raise a sail on a sailboat?

4. **COMMUNICATE** Write a paragraph or label a diagram that explains how a wheel and axle is a type of lever.

5. **CRITICAL THINKING** *Evaluate* Give an example of a simple machine. How does this simple machine make work easier?

WHY IT MATTERS THINK ABOUT IT
How many times do you lift things during the day? What sort of things do you lift?

WHY IT MATTERS WRITE ABOUT IT
How do your arms, legs, and fingers help you lift things?

113

SCIENCE MAGAZINE

A Music

Can people make music with simple machines? Sure they can! A piano isn't just a musical instrument, it's a machine full of levers!

Press any piano key and you push down on one end of a lever. The other end is inside the piano. It's attached to a small hammer that's covered in soft felt. When the end of this lever goes up, it hits the hammer against the metal strings for that note. The strings begin to vibrate. You hear a musical note!

Take your finger off the key. A pad called a damper touches the strings. They stop vibrating and the sound stops!

A piano has 88 keys and more than 200 strings. Some hammers strike three strings at one time. Short strings make high sounds. Long strings make low sounds.

The first piano was made in 1709 by Bartolomeo Cristofori of Italy. He called the instrument *piano e forte*. That means "soft and loud" in Italian. Before long Cristofori's invention became known as the piano.

Wolfgang Amadeus Mozart was an expert on a piano's levers. Born in Austria in 1756, Mozart wrote some of the world's most important piano music. Ludwig van Beethoven was born in Germany in 1770. He followed in Mozart's footsteps and also wrote great piano music.

DISCUSSION STARTER

1. Which piano part on the outside is a lever? Which part on the inside is a lever?
2. Is playing the piano a form of work? How do you know?

Music Link

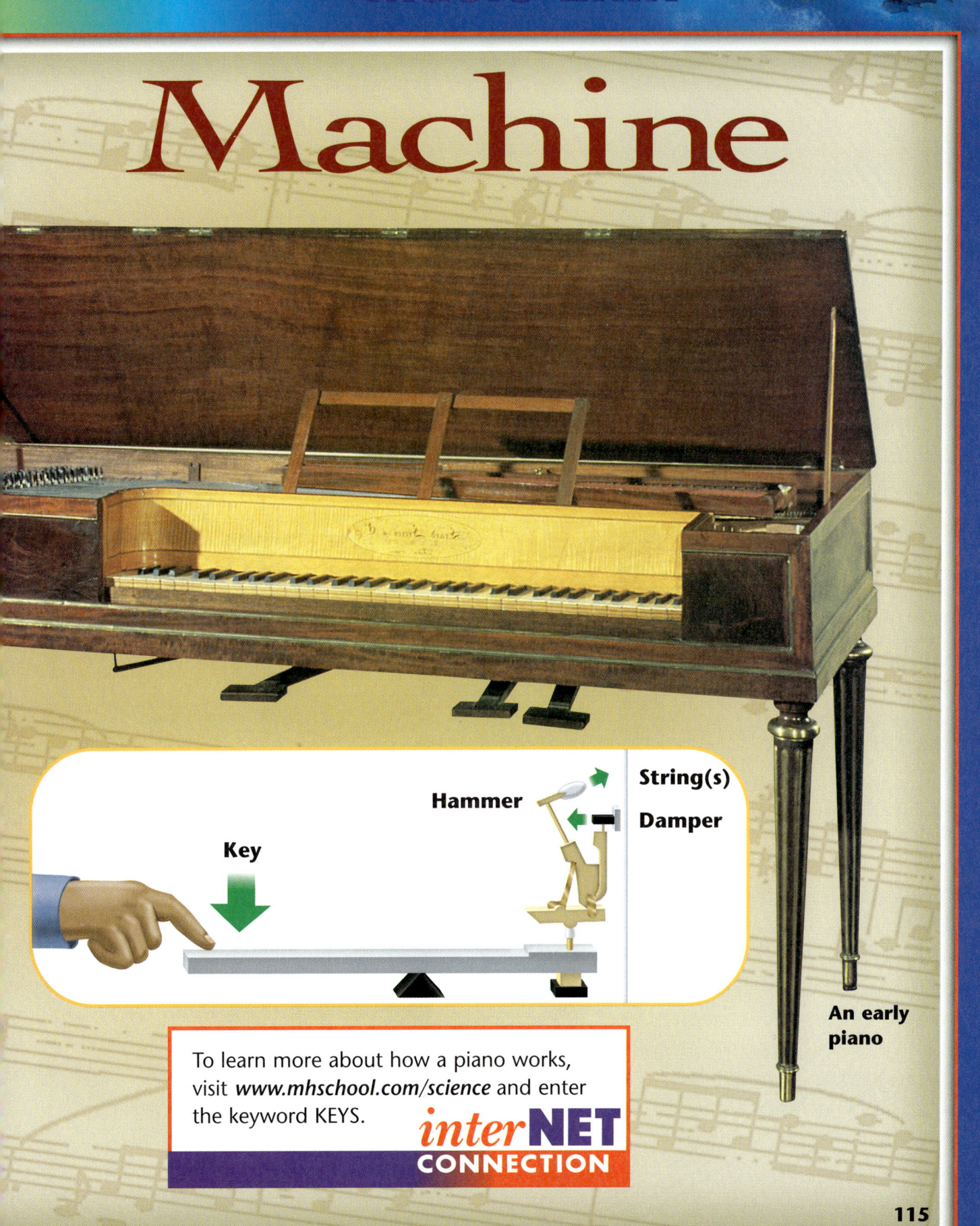

Machine

Key · **Hammer** · **String(s)** · **Damper**

An early piano

To learn more about how a piano works, visit *www.mhschool.com/science* and enter the keyword KEYS.

interNET CONNECTION

115

Topic 6
PHYSICAL SCIENCE

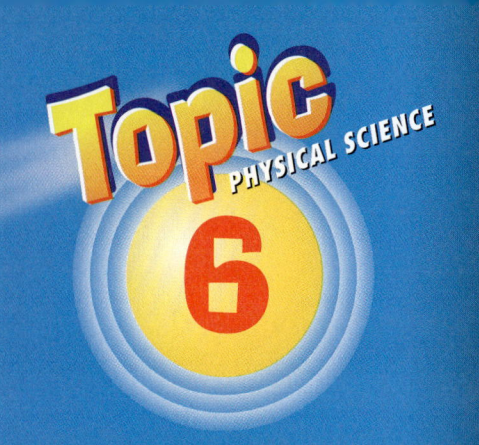

WHY IT MATTERS

Simple machines can make small jobs and big jobs less of a chore!

SCIENCE WORDS

inclined plane a flat surface that is raised at one end

wedge two inclined planes placed back to back

screw an inclined plane wrapped into a spiral

compound machine two or more simple machines put together

More Simple Machines

This pyramid, called the Pyramid of the Sun, was built over a thousand years ago. Made from mud, dirt, and large pieces of stone, it stands over 200 feet tall. A thousand years ago there were no bulldozers, tractors, or trucks. Somehow people moved large stones and other material hundreds of feet off the ground. How did they do it?

EXPLORE

HYPOTHESIZE When people built pyramids many years ago, they may have used a ramp to help them move rocks. How can a ramp make work easier? Write a hypothesis in your *Science Journal*. How might you test your ideas?

EXPLORE ACTIVITY

Investigate How a Ramp Can Make Work Easier

Evaluate how a ramp can make work easier.

MATERIALS
- 1 meter wooden board
- spring scale
- thin spiral notebook
- 30 cm piece of string
- chair
- meter stick
- safety goggles
- *Science Journal*

PROCEDURES

Safety: Wear goggles.

1. Lean one end of the wooden board on the chair. Tie one end of the string around the bottom of the spring scale and the other end to the middle of the spiral wire of the notebook.

2. **MEASURE** Measure the pull needed to lift the notebook straight up to the height of the chair's seat. Then measure the distance you pulled the book. Record your measurements in your *Science Journal*.

3. **MEASURE** Measure the pull needed to move the notebook up the board to the seat of the chair. Then measure the distance you pulled the book. Record your measurements.

4. **EXPERIMENT** Adjust the board so it is at a steeper angle. Repeat step 3.

CONCLUDE AND APPLY

1. **INTERPRET DATA** Look at your measurements. Which method of moving the notebook required more force? Which method required moving the notebook a greater distance?

2. **COMPARE** Think about the three methods. What is the advantage of each one? What is the disadvantage?

GOING FURTHER: Apply

3. **EVALUATE** Which method would you use to put a stuffed animal onto a shelf? Which method would you use to put a bike into a truck?

117

How Can a Ramp Make Work Easier?

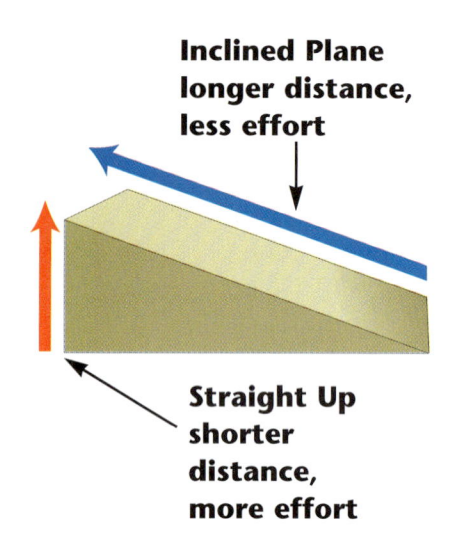

Inclined Plane longer distance, less effort

Straight Up shorter distance, more effort

How did the people who built the Pyramid of the Sun lift blocks of stone so high in the air? They may have used ramps. A ramp is an example of an **inclined plane** (in klīnd′ plān). An inclined plane is a flat surface that is raised at one end. The Explore Activity shows that inclined planes are simple machines that make work easier.

How does an inclined plane make work easier? Going up a hill, you have two paths. The path that goes straight up is shorter. However, it takes more effort. The ramp is a longer distance, but it takes less effort.

Which way should you go? When the object isn't heavy, you may choose to go straight up. When the object is heavy, you must take the ramp. The stone blocks that the people used to build the Pyramid of the Sun were too heavy to move straight up. Scientists think that they may have moved them on an inclined plane.

How do ramps make work easier for these people? Where have you seen ramps used in your community?

118

What Kind of Simple Machine Is a Plow?

A **wedge** (wej) is another simple machine. A wedge is made of two inclined planes placed back to back. A wedge uses force to raise an object up or split objects apart.

An ax is a wedge. When an ax is swung, the downward force of the ax is changed into a sideways force. The sideways force splits the wood apart.

Another example of a wedge is a plow. A plow is a machine used by farmers. As the plow is dragged through the soil, it cuts through the ground. The soil is moved aside.

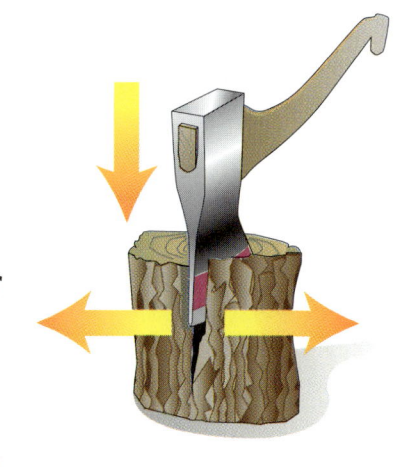

The downward force of the ax changes to the sideways force that splits the wood.

A plow helps a farmer prepare the ground for planting.

What Is a Screw?

What happens when you wrap an inclined plane around a pole? You have a **screw** (skrü)! A screw is an inclined plane wrapped into a spiral. The ridges of the screw are called threads.

A screw with a longer inclined plane has more threads. A screw with a shorter inclined plane has fewer threads.

READING DIAGRAMS

1. **REPRESENT** Where is the inclined plane on a screw?
2. **DISCUSS** Which screw has a longer inclined plane? How do you know?

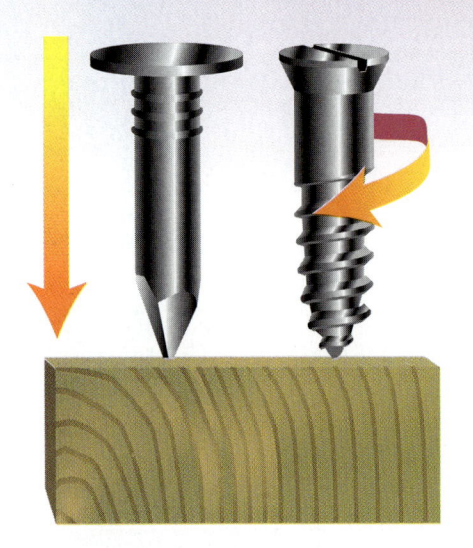

It takes less force to turn a screw than to pound a nail. That is because the screw is moving a longer distance. When you turn the head of the screw once, the spiral part of the screw travels a long way. You apply force over a longer distance, just like any other inclined plane. The longer the distance, the less force you need to do work.

SKILL BUILDER

Skill: Using Numbers

MATERIALS
- *Science Journal*
- ruler

EVALUATING DIFFERENCES

You know that a screw is a simple machine that makes work easier. A screw makes work easier just like any other inclined plane—by letting you use less force over a greater distance. Screws come in many shapes and sizes. Some screws make work easier than others. How can one screw make work easier than another?

The diagram below shows three screws. In this activity you will use numbers to evaluate how each screw is different. Then you will use that information to infer which screw makes work the easiest.

PROCEDURES

1. **MEASURE** What is the width of the head of each screw? What is the length of each screw? Record your measurements in the table in your *Science Journal*.

2. **USE NUMBERS** What is the number of threads on each screw? Record the information in the table.

CONCLUDE AND APPLY

1. **COMPARE** How does the width and length of each screw compare? How does the number of threads on each screw compare?

2. **EXPLAIN** How does the number of threads on each screw relate to the length of its inclined plane?

3. **INFER** Which screw makes the work easiest? How do you know?

What Happens if You Put Two Simple Machines Together?

You can make your work easier by using a **compound machine** (kom′ pound mə shēn′), too. When you put two or more simple machines together, you make a compound machine. A pair of scissors is a compound machine. Part of a pair of scissors is a lever. Part of a pair of scissors is a wedge. Can you tell which part is which?

A water faucet is also a compound machine. Which part of the water faucet is a wheel and axle? Which part is a screw?

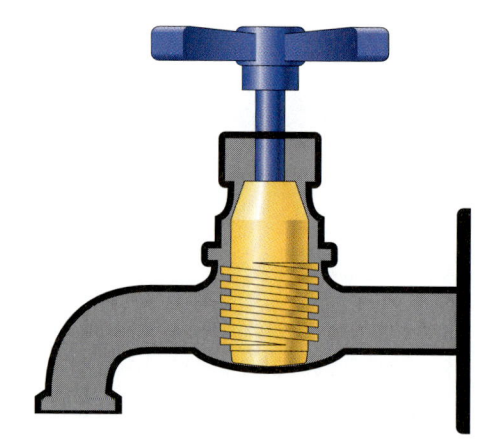

A bicycle uses wheels and axles and a lever. There are several sets of wheels and axles. Can you find them all? Can you find the lever?

Brain Power

Design your own compound machine. It should be made of two or more simple machines. What does your compound machine do? How does it work?

WHY IT MATTERS

Simple and compound machines help you do many of your everyday activities. They help you do things like cut an apple for lunch, wrap a birthday present for a friend, travel from place to place, and wash up before bed!

What compound machine is this girl using? What simple machines make it up?

REVIEW

1. How does an inclined plane make work easier?
2. What is a compound machine?
3. Draw a picture of a knife cutting a banana. In what direction does the knife apply force? In what direction does the banana move?
4. **USE NUMBERS** You have two screws. Each measures 2 inches long and has a 1-inch head. Screw A has 20 threads. Screw B has 30. Which screw will make work easier? How do you know?
5. **CRITICAL THINKING** *Apply* Where is the inclined plane on a screw? Draw or write an explanation.

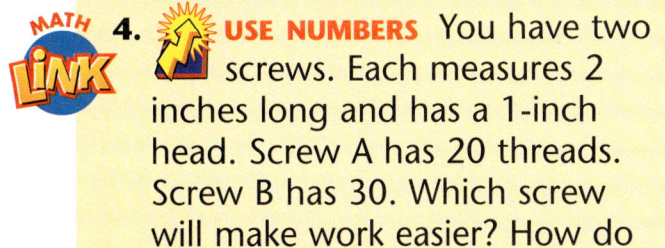

WHY IT MATTERS THINK ABOUT IT What simple or compound machine have you used today? How did the machine help you?

WHY IT MATTERS WRITE ABOUT IT What if the machine you used today did not exist. How would you have done the work you needed to do? How much harder would the work have been?

READING SKILL Look at page 122. How many compound machines are listed on this page? Choose one of the compound machines. What simple machines make it up? Make a list.

SCIENCE MAGAZINE

A Closer Look

SIMPLE MACHINES on a PLAYGROUND

Push off! Wheeee, you're high in the air. Then down you come. Up and down you go on a simple machine . . . a seesaw! You don't think about working a machine. You're having too much fun!

Can you find the fulcrum of a lever in the picture? Hint: Look under the seesaw. Each person sits on one end of a lever. That lever makes it easy to move up and down.

Did you notice that the ramp is an inclined plane?

This simple machine makes it easy for someone in a wheelchair to play with friends. Without a ramp, it would take several people to lift the wheelchair up the stairs. Rolling up the ramp is easier. A child can do it without help!

DISCUSSION STARTER

Where have you seen ramps? You're going to seesaw with a friend. You both weigh the same. The fulcrum is in the middle. Draw how the seesaw will look when you get on.

To learn more about simple machines, visit **www.mhschool.com/science** and enter the keyword RAMP.

interNET CONNECTION

124

CHAPTER 4 REVIEW

SCIENCE WORDS

compound machine p.122
energy p.101
inclined plane p.118
lever p.109
machine p.108
pulley p.112
screw p.120
simple machine p.109
wedge p.119
wheel and axle p.111
work p.100

USING SCIENCE WORDS

Number a paper from 1 to 10. Fill in 1 to 5 with words from the list above

1. An inclined plane wrapped into a spiral is a(n) __?__.
2. Pulleys and wheels and axles are both __?__.
3. When you use a force to change the motion of an object, you do __?__.
4. The simple machine with a fulcrum, load, and force is a(n) __?__.
5. A machine with few or no moving parts is a(n) __?__.
6–10. **Pick five words from the list above. Include all words that were not used in 1 to 5. Write each word in a sentence.**

UNDERSTANDING SCIENCE IDEAS

11. How does an inclined plane make work easier?
12. What is the difference between stored energy and energy of motion?

USING IDEAS AND SKILLS

13. **READING SKILL: RECOGNIZE A LIST** Look at the ramps and their measurements. List them in order from longest to shortest.

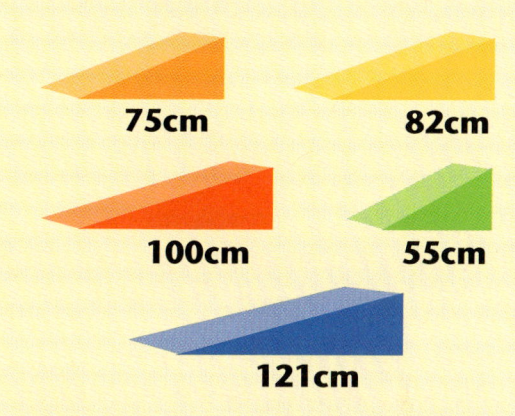

75cm   82cm
100cm   55cm
121cm

14. **USE NUMBERS** Look at your list from question 13. Which ramp makes work easiest? How do you know?

15. **THINKING LIKE A SCIENTIST** You are asked to explain how a lever makes work easier to a class of third-grade students. What will you tell them? Design a poster to help illustrate your ideas.

PROBLEMS and PUZZLES

Whee! Remember the rides at an amusement park? Machines moved you up, down, and around. Use what you've learned about machines and forces to build your own amusement park. You can use materials such as rubber bands, paper plates, milk cartons, and crayons.

125

UNIT 2 REVIEW

SCIENCE WORDS

energy p.101
force p.78
friction p.90
gravity p.80
inclined plane p.118
lever p.109
motion p.70
position p.68
pulley p.112
screw p.120
speed p.71
wedge p.119
weight p.81
wheel and axle p.111
work p.100

USING SCIENCE WORDS

Number a paper from 1 to 10. Beside each number write the word or term that best completes the sentence.

1. When you squeeze the brakes, the force that slows the bike is __?__.

2. How fast a car is moving is called its __?__.

3. An apple falling from a tree is pulled by a force called __?__.

4. A car that changes position is in __?__.

5. You can find the pull of gravity on your body by finding your __?__.

6. The machine made from a wheel and a rope is called a(n) __?__.

7. You are standing with your leg ready to kick a soccer ball. Your leg has __?__.

8. When you kick the soccer ball and make it roll, you are doing __?__.

9. A ramp is a kind of __?__.

10. A seesaw is an example of a __?__.

UNDERSTANDING SCIENCE IDEAS

Write 11 to 15. For each number write the letter for the best answer. You may wish to use the hints provided.

11. Which of the following could be the speed of a car?
    a. 30 miles
    b. 30 miles per hour
    c. 30 hours
    d. 30 meters

    (Hint: Read page 71.)

12. The Moon has less matter than Earth. Which is true? You:
    a. are shorter on the Moon
    b. are heavier on the Moon
    c. are heavier on Earth
    d. weigh the same on both

    (Hint: Read page 82.)

13. Very smooth playground slides
    a. decrease friction
    b. decrease speed
    c. decrease motion
    d. decrease weight

    (Hint: Read pages 90–91.)

14. In science, work occurs when a force causes a change in motion. Which is true? Work
    a. takes money
    b. takes a long time
    c. changes an object's size
    d. changes an object's position

    (Hint: Read page 100.)

15. Which simple machine lets a roller skate roll?
    a. a screw
    b. a pulley
    c. an inclined plane
    d. a wheel and axle

    (Hint: Read page 111.)

UNIT 2 REVIEW

USING IDEAS AND SKILLS

16. A woman walks one block in two minutes. Another woman walks the same block in eight minutes. Who has the greater speed? Explain.

17. What happens when you hang a weight on a spring scale?

18. **INTERPRETING DATA** Look at the graph below. How does the kind of surface that a ball is on affect how far the ball rolls?

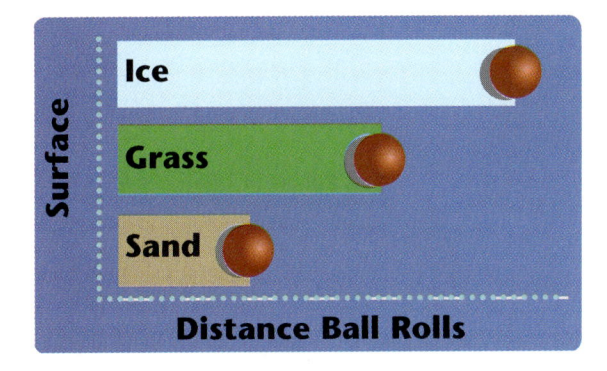

Surface / Ice / Grass / Sand / Distance Ball Rolls

19. Give an example of the work you do at home and explain why it is work to a scientist.

THINKING LIKE A SCIENTIST

20. **USE NUMBERS** You want to pry a big rock out of your garden. You have a 4-foot board and a 6-foot board. Which board will help you move the rock more easily? Explain.

interNET CONNECTION

For help in reviewing this unit, visit www.mhschool.com/science

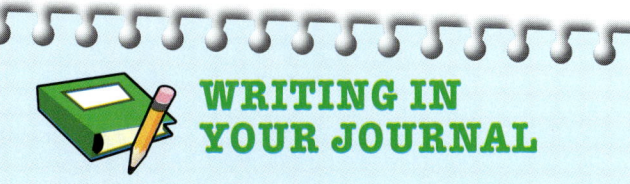

WRITING IN YOUR JOURNAL

SCIENCE IN YOUR LIFE
List three ways you use levers every day. Use the list to write a description of how machines are important to you.

PRODUCT ADS
Advertisements sometimes show people jumping very, very high in a certain type of sneakers. What force are these advertisements ignoring? Explain your answer.

HOW SCIENTISTS WORK
In this unit you learned about machines and how they make work easier. Tell why you think it is important for scientists to do experiments to learn about machines.

Design your own Experiment

Think of a way to make a lever that will lift the front of a chair one inch above the floor. The chair should be touched only by the lever. Review your experiment with your teacher before you carry it out.

UNIT 2 REVIEW

PROBLEMS and PUZZLES

Lever-Gram Puzzles

Tell what you think will happen in each lever-gram. Will the lever move? If so, which way?

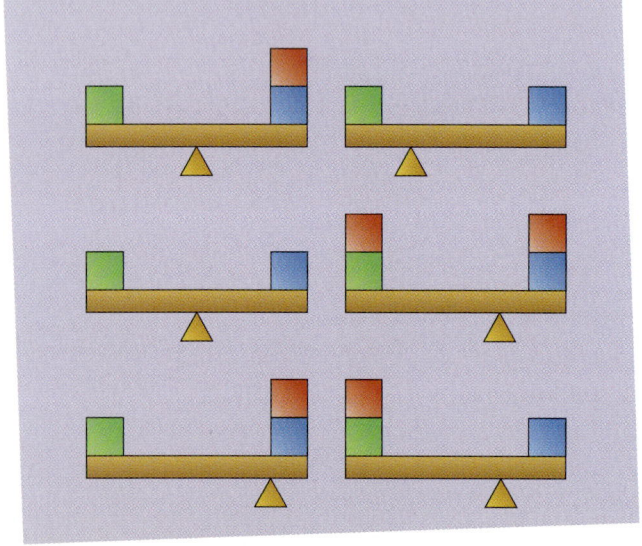

Amanda's Pulley Problem

Amanda can lift 10 kilograms with a single pulley. What kind of pulley system will she need to lift a greater load? Draw a picture of it.

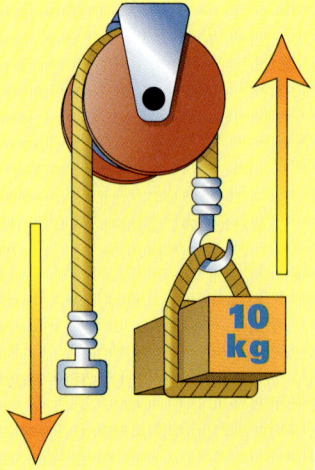

Trucking Troubles!

THE PROBLEM

Brontosaurus Trucks are the biggest trucks on the road! The trucks are so big that drivers complain that their steering wheels are hard to turn. Can you think of a way to make steering a Bronto easier?

HYPOTHESIZE

Decide what you could do to make the steering wheel of a Bronto Truck turn more easily. How would you change the steering wheel? Why do you think your idea would work? Include a drawing of your design.

REFERENCE SECTION

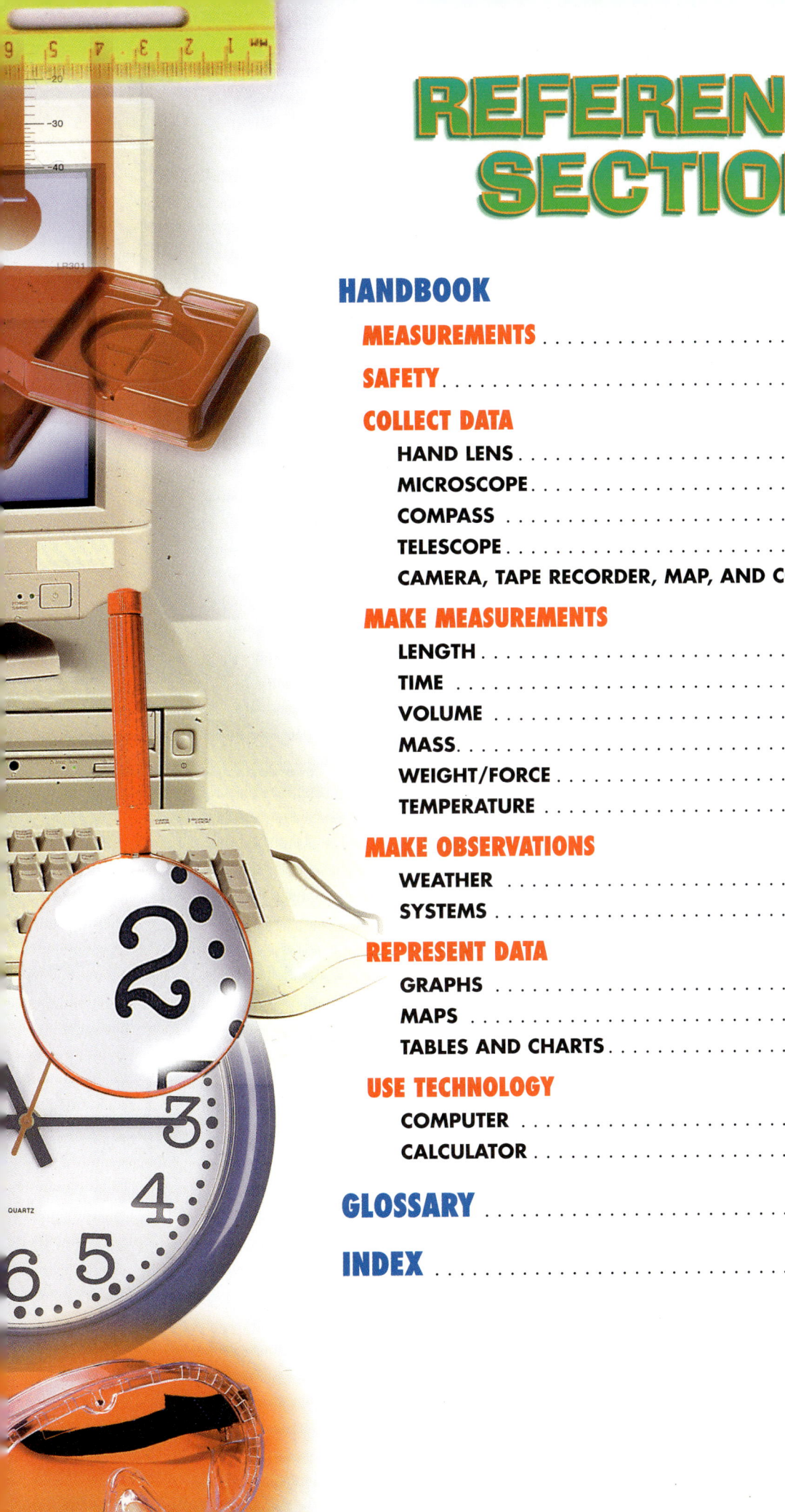

HANDBOOK

MEASUREMENTS ... R2
SAFETY ... R4
COLLECT DATA
- HAND LENS ... R6
- MICROSCOPE ... R7
- COMPASS ... R8
- TELESCOPE ... R9
- CAMERA, TAPE RECORDER, MAP, AND COMPASS ... R10

MAKE MEASUREMENTS
- LENGTH ... R11
- TIME ... R12
- VOLUME ... R13
- MASS ... R14
- WEIGHT/FORCE ... R16
- TEMPERATURE ... R17

MAKE OBSERVATIONS
- WEATHER ... R18
- SYSTEMS ... R19

REPRESENT DATA
- GRAPHS ... R20
- MAPS ... R22
- TABLES AND CHARTS ... R23

USE TECHNOLOGY
- COMPUTER ... R24
- CALCULATOR ... R26

GLOSSARY ... R27

INDEX ... R39

MEASUREMENTS

Temperature

1. The temperature is 77 degrees Fahrenheit.

2. That is the same as 25 degrees Celsius.

3. Water boils at 212 degrees Fahrenheit.

4. Water freezes at 0 degrees Celsius.

Length and Area

1. This classroom is 10 meters wide and 20 meters long.

2. That means the area is 200 square meters.

Mass and Weight

1. That baseball bat weighs 32 ounces.

2. 32 ounces is the same as 2 pounds.

3. The mass of the bat is 907 grams.

Volume of Fluids

1. This bottle of juice has a volume of 1 liter.
2. That is a little more than 1 quart.

Weight/Force

I weigh 85 pounds. That is a force of 380.8 newtons.

Rate

1. She can walk 20 meters in 5 seconds.
2. That means her speed is 4 meters per second.

Table of Measurements

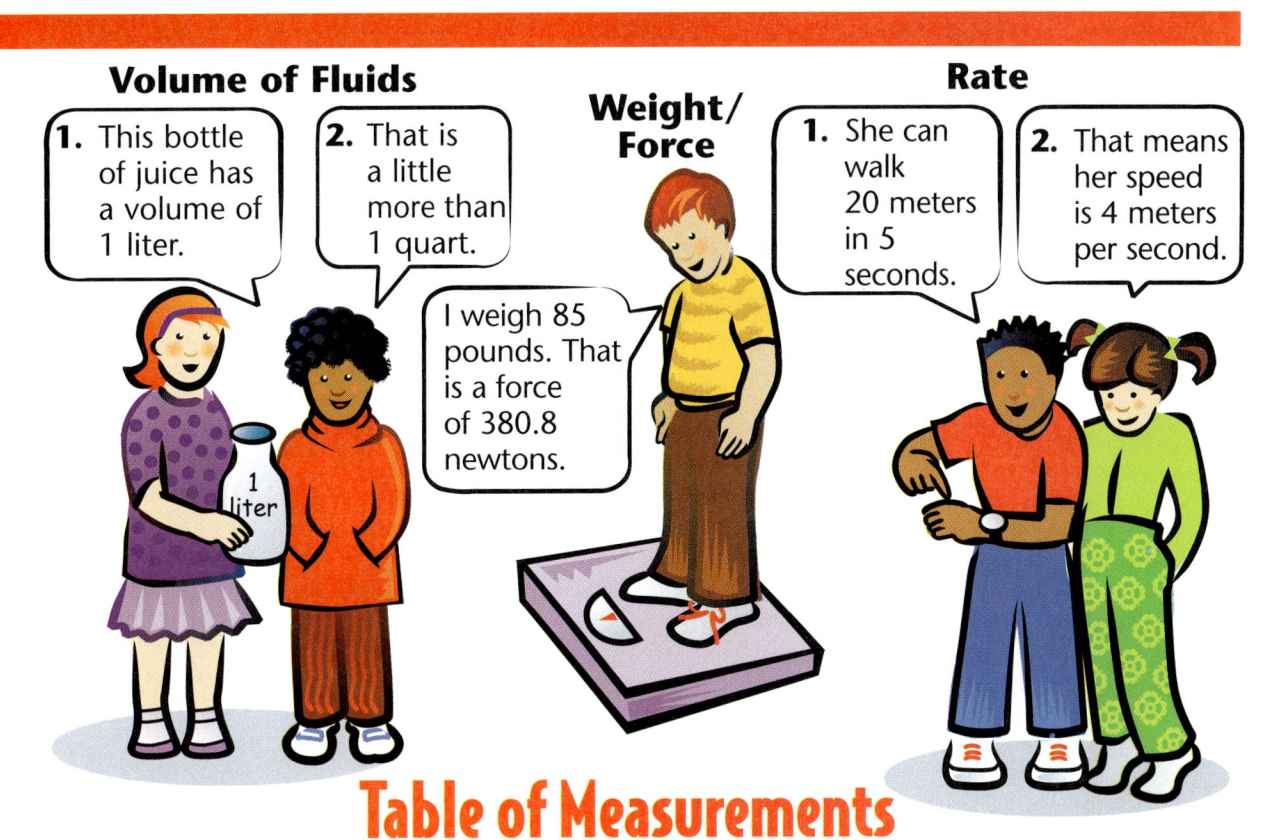

SI (International System) of Units	English System of Units
Temperature Water freezes at 0 degrees Celsius (°C) and boils at 100°C.	**Temperature** Water freezes at 32 degrees Fahrenheit (°F) and boils at 212°F.
Length and Distance 10 millimeters (mm) = 1 centimeter (cm) 100 centimeters = 1 meter (m) 1,000 meters = 1 kilometer (km)	**Length and Distance** 12 inches (in.) = 1 foot (ft) 3 feet = 1 yard (yd) 5,280 feet = 1 mile (mi)
Volume 1 cubic centimeter (cm^3) = 1 milliliter (mL) 1,000 milliliters = 1 liter (L)	**Volume of Fluids** 8 fluid ounces (fl oz) = 1 cup (c) 2 cups = 1 pint (pt) 2 pints = 1 quart (qt) 4 quarts = 1 gallon (gal)
Mass 1,000 milligrams (mg) = 1 gram (g) 1,000 grams = 1 kilogram (kg)	**Weight** 16 ounces (oz) = 1 pound (lb) 2,000 pounds = 1 ton (T)
Area 1 square kilometer (km^2) = 1 km x 1 km 1 hectare = 10,000 square meters (m^2)	**Rate** mph = miles per hour
Rate m/s = meters per second km/h = kilometers per hour	
Force 1 newton (N) = 1 kg x m/s^2	

SAFETY

In the Classroom

The most important part of doing any experiment is doing it safely. You can be safe by paying attention to your teacher and doing your work carefully. Here are some other ways to stay safe while you do experiments.

Before the Experiment

- Read all of the directions. Make sure you understand them. When you see ▧, be sure to follow the safety rule.
- Listen to your teacher for special safety directions. If you don't understand something, ask for help.
- Wash your hands with soap and water before an activity.

During the Experiment

- Wear safety goggles when your teacher tells you to wear them and whenever you see 🥽. Wear goggles when working with something that can fly into your eyes
- Wear splash-proof goggles when working with liquids.
- Wear a safety apron if you work with anything messy or anything that might spill.

- If you spill something, wipe it up right away or ask your teacher for help.
- Tell your teacher if something breaks. If glass breaks do not clean it up yourself.
- Keep your hair and clothes away from open flames. Tie back long hair and roll up long sleeves.

- Be careful around a hot plate. Know when it is on and when it is off. Remember that the plate stays hot for a few minutes after you turn it off.
- Keep your hands dry around electrical equipment.
- Don't eat or drink anything during the experiment.

After the Experiment

- Put equipment back the way your teacher tells you.
- Dispose of things the way your teacher tells you.
- Clean up your work area and wash your hands with soap and water.

In the Field

- Always be accompanied by a trusted adult—like your teacher or a parent or guardian.
- Never touch animals or plants without the adult's approval. The animal might bite. The plant might be poison ivy or another dangerous plant.

Responsibility

Acting safely is one way to be responsible. You can also be responsible by treating animals, the environment, and each other with respect in the class and in the field.

Treat Living Things with Respect

- If you have animals in the classroom, keep their homes clean. Change the water in fish tanks and clean out cages.
- Feed classroom animals the right amounts of food.
- Give your classroom animals enough space.
- When you observe animals, don't hurt them or disturb their homes.
- Find a way to care for animals while school is on vacation.

Treat the Environment with Respect

- Do not pick flowers.
- Do not litter, including gum and food.
- If you see litter, ask your teacher if you can pick it up.
- Recycle materials used in experiments. Ask your teacher what materials can be recycled instead of thrown away. These might include plastics, aluminum, and newspapers.

Treat Each Other with Respect

- Use materials carefully around others so that people don't get hurt or get stains on their clothes.
- Be careful not to bump people when they are doing experiments. Do not disturb or damage their experiments.
- If you see that people are having trouble with an experiment, help them.

COLLECT DATA

Use a Hand Lens

You use a hand lens to magnify an object, or make the object look larger. With a hand lens, you can see details that would be hard to see without the hand lens.

Magnify a Piece of Cereal

1. Place a piece of your favorite cereal on a flat surface. Look at the cereal carefully. Draw a picture of it.
2. Hold the hand lens so that it is just above the cereal. Look through the lens, and slowly move it away from the cereal. The cereal will look larger.
3. Keep moving the hand lens until the cereal begins to look blurry. Then move the lens a little closer to the cereal until you can see it clearly.
4. Draw a picture of the cereal as you see it through the hand lens. Fill in details that you did not see before.
5. Repeat this activity using objects you are studying in science. It might be a rock, some soil, a flower, a seed, or something else.

Use a Microscope

Hand lenses make objects look several times larger. A microscope, however, can magnify an object to look hundreds of times larger.

Examine Salt Grains

1. Place the microscope on a flat surface. Always carry a microscope with both hands. Hold the arm with one hand, and put your other hand beneath the base.
2. Look at the drawing to learn the different parts of the microscope.
3. Move the mirror so that it reflects light up toward the stage. Never point the mirror directly at the Sun or a bright light. Bright light can cause permanent eye damage.
4. Place a few grains of salt on the slide. Put the slide under the stage clips on the stage. Be sure that the salt grains are over the hole in the stage.
5. Look through the eyepiece. Turn the focusing knob slowly until the salt grains come into focus.
6. Draw what the grains look like through the microscope.
7. Look at other objects through the microscope. Try a piece of leaf, a strand of human hair, or a pencil mark.
8. Draw what each object looks like through the microscope. Do any of the objects look alike? If so, how? Are any of the objects alive? How do you know?

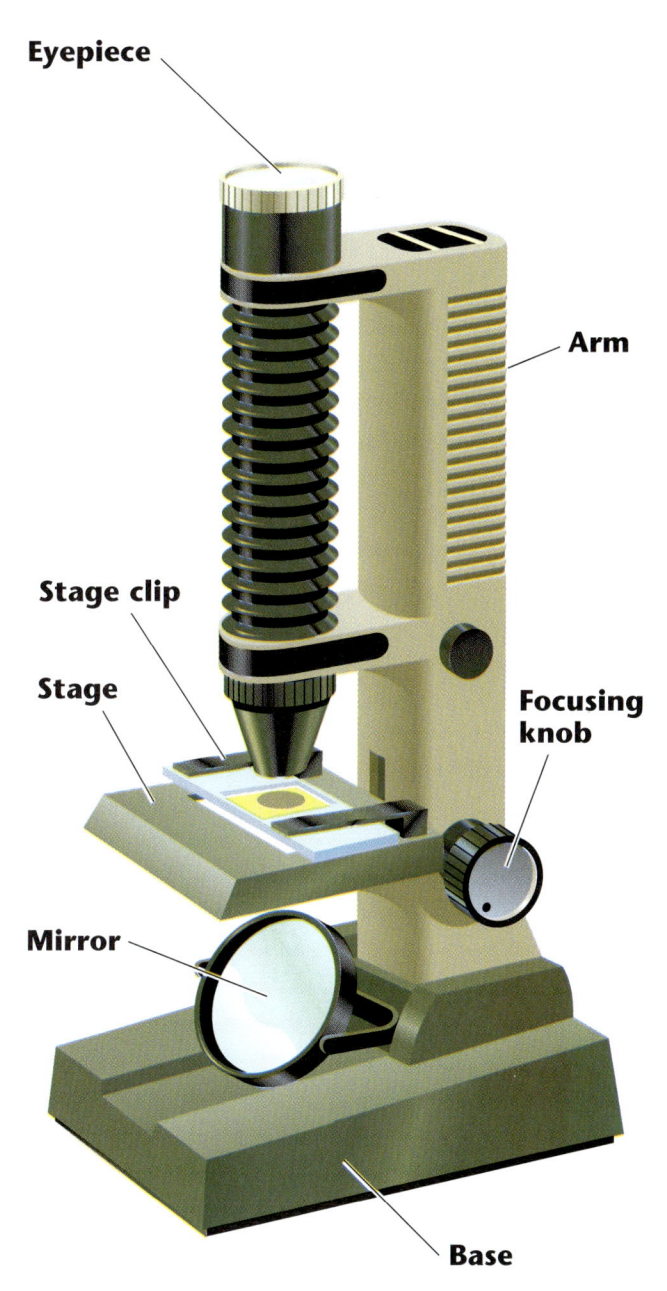

COLLECT DATA

Use a Compass

You use a compass to find directions. A compass is a small, thin magnet that swings freely, like a spinner in a board game. One end of the magnet always points north. This end is the magnet's north pole. How does a compass work?

1. Place the compass on a surface that is not made of magnetic material. A wooden table or a sidewalk works well.
2. Find the magnet's north pole. The north pole is marked in some way, usually with a color or an arrowhead.
3. Notice the letters *N, E, S,* and *W* on the compass. These letters stand for the directions north, east, south, and west. When the magnet stops swinging, turn the compass so that the *N* lines up with the north pole of the magnet.
4. Face to the north. Then face to the east, to the south, and to the west.
5. Repeat this activity by holding the compass in your hand and then at different places indoors and outdoors.

Use a Telescope

A telescope makes faraway objects, like the Moon, look larger. A telescope also lets you see stars that are too faint to see with just your eyes.

Look at the Moon

1. Look at the Moon in the night sky. Draw a picture of what you see. Draw as many details as you can.
2. Point a telescope toward the Moon. Look through the eyepiece of the telescope. Move the telescope until you see the Moon. Turn the knob until the Moon comes into focus.
3. Draw a picture of what you see. Include details. Compare your two pictures.

Look at the Stars

1. Find the brightest star in the sky. Notice if there are any other stars near it.
2. Point a telescope toward the brightest star. Look through the eyepiece and turn the knob until the stars come into focus. Move the telescope until you find the brightest star.
3. Can you see stars through the telescope that you cannot see with just your eyes?

COLLECT DATA

Use a Camera, Tape Recorder, Map, and Compass

Camera

You can use a camera to record what you observe in nature. Keep these tips in mind.

1. Hold the camera steady. Gently press the button so that you do not jerk the camera.
2. Try to take pictures with the Sun at your back. Then your pictures will be bright and clear.
3. Don't get too close to the subject. Without a special lens, the picture could turn out blurry.
4. Be patient. If you are taking a picture of an animal, you may have to wait for the animal to appear.

Tape Recorder

You can record observations on a tape recorder. This is sometimes better than writing notes because a tape recorder can record your observations at the exact time you are making them. Later you can listen to the tape and write down your observations.

Map and Compass

When you are busy observing nature, it might be easy to get lost. You can use a map of the area and a compass to find your way. Here are some tips.

1. Lightly mark on the map your starting place. It might be the place where the bus parked.
2. Always know where you are on the map compared to your starting place. Watch for landmarks on the map, such as a river, a pond, trails, or buildings.
3. Use the map and compass to find special places to observe, such as a pond. Look at the map to see which direction the place is from you. Hold the compass to see where that direction is.
4. Use your map and compass with a friend.

R10

MAKE MEASUREMENTS

Length

Find Length with a Ruler

1. Look at this section of a ruler. Each centimeter is divided into 10 millimeters. How long is the paper clip?
2. The length of the paper clip is 3 centimeters plus 2 millimeters. You can write this length as 3.2 centimeters.
3. Place the ruler on your desk. Lay a pencil against the ruler so that one end of the pencil lines up with the left edge of the ruler. Record the length of the pencil.
4. Trade your pencil with a classmate. Measure and record the length of each other's pencils. Compare your answers.

Measuring Area

Area is the amount of surface something covers. To find the area of a rectangle, multiply the rectangle's length by its width. For example, the rectangle here is 3 centimeters long and 2 centimeters wide. Its area is 3 cm x 2 cm = 6 square centimeters. You write the area as 6 cm^2.

1. Find the area of your science book. Measure the book's length to the nearest centimeter. Measure its width.
2. Multiply the book's length by its width. Remember to put the answer in cm^2.

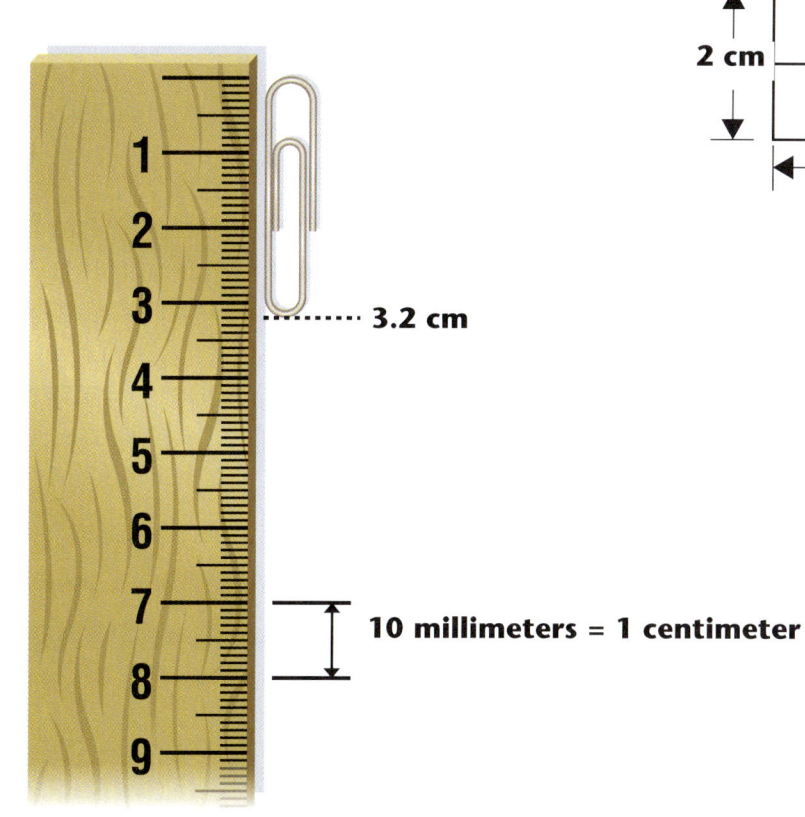

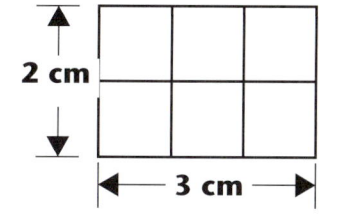

3.2 cm

10 millimeters = 1 centimeter

2 cm

3 cm

R11

MAKE MEASUREMENTS

Time

You use timing devices to measure how long something takes to happen. Some timing devices you use in science are a clock with a second hand and a stopwatch. Which one is more accurate?

Comparing a Clock and a Stopwatch

1. Look at a clock with a second hand. The second hand is the hand that you can see moving. It measures seconds.
2. Get an egg timer with falling sand or some device like a windup toy that runs down after a certain length of time. When the second hand of the clock points to 12, tell your partner to start the egg timer. Watch the clock while the sand in the egg timer is falling.
3. When the sand stops falling, count how many seconds it took. Record this measurement. Repeat the activity, and compare the two measurements.
4. Switch roles with your partner.
5. Look at a stopwatch. Click the button on the top right. This starts the time. Click the button again. This stops the time. Click the button on the top left. This sets the stopwatch back to zero. Notice that the stopwatch tells time in hours, minutes, seconds, and hundredths of a second.
6. Repeat the activity in steps 1–3, but use the stopwatch instead of a clock. Make sure the stopwatch is set to zero. Click the top right button to start timing.

Click the button again when the sand stops falling. Make sure you and your partner time the sand twice.

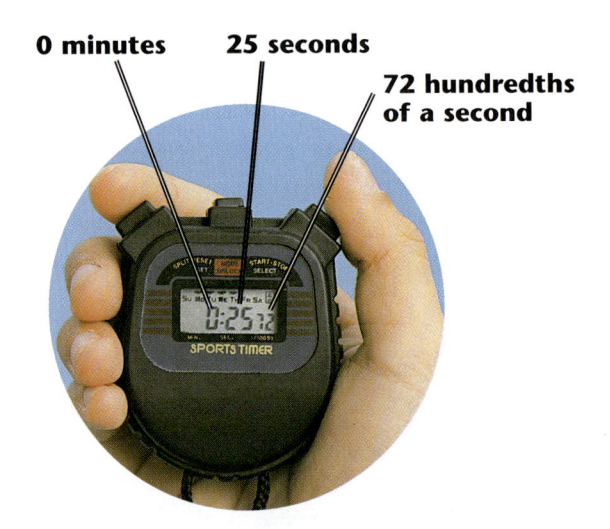

0 minutes **25 seconds**
72 hundredths of a second

More About Time

1. Use the stopwatch to time how long it takes an ice cube to melt under cold running water. How long does an ice cube take to melt under warm running water?
2. Match each of these times with the action you think took that amount of time.

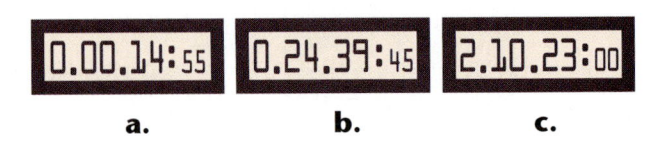

0.00.14:55	0.24.39:45	2.10.23:00
a.	b.	c.

1. A Little League baseball game
2. Saying the Pledge of Allegiance
3. Recess

R12

Volume

Have you ever used a measuring cup? Measuring cups measure the volume of liquids. Volume is the amount of space something takes up. To bake a cake, you might measure the volume of water, vegetable oil, or melted butter. In science you use special measuring cups called beakers and graduated cylinders. These containers are marked in milliliters (mL).

Measure the Volume of a Liquid

1. Look at the beaker and at the graduated cylinder. The beaker has marks for each 25 mL up to 200 mL. The graduated cylinder has marks for each 1 mL up to 100 mL.
2. The surface of the water in the graduated cylinder curves up at the sides. You measure the volume by reading the height of the water at the flat part. What is the volume of water in the graduated cylinder? How much water is in the beaker? They both contain 75 mL of water.
3. Pour 50 mL of water from a pitcher into a graduated cylinder. The water should be at the 50-mL mark on the graduated cylinder. If you go over the mark, pour a little water back into the pitcher.
4. Pour the 50 mL of water into a beaker.
5. Repeat steps 3 and 4 using 30 mL, 45 mL, and 25 mL of water.
6. Measure the volume of water you have in the beaker. Do you have about the same amount of water as your classmates?

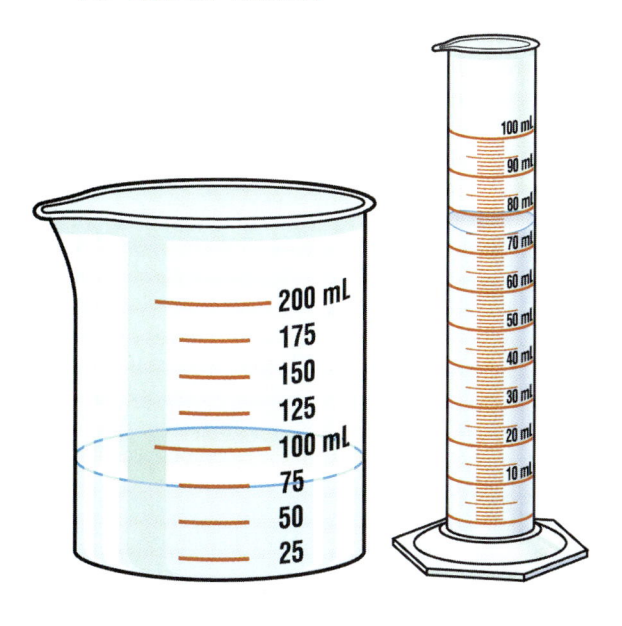

MAKE MEASUREMENTS

Mass

Mass is the amount of matter an object has. You use a balance to measure mass. To find the mass of an object, you balance it with objects whose masses you know. Let's find the mass of a box of crayons.

Measure the Mass of a Box of Crayons

1. Place the balance on a flat, level surface. Check that the two pans are empty and clean.
2. Make sure the empty pans are balanced with each other. The pointer should point to the middle mark. If it does not, move the slider a little to the right or left to balance the pans.
3. Gently place a box of crayons on the left pan. The pan will drop lower.
4. Add masses to the right pan until the pans are balanced. You can use paper clips.
5. Count the number of paper clips that are in the right pan. Two paper clips equal about one gram. What is the mass of the box of crayons? Record the number. After the number, write a *g* for "grams."

R14

Predict the Mass of More Crayons

1. Leave the box of crayons and the masses on the balance.
2. Get two more crayons. If you put them in the pan with the box of crayons, what do you think the mass of all the crayons will be? Write down what you predict the total mass will be.
3. Check your prediction. Gently place the two crayons in the left pan. Add masses, such as paper clips, to the right pan until the pans are balanced.
4. Calculate the mass as you did before. Record this number. How close is it to your prediction?

More About Mass

What was the mass of all your crayons? It was probably less than 100 grams. What would happen if you replaced the crayons with a pineapple? You may not have enough masses to balance the pineapple. It has a mass of about 1,000 grams. That's the same as 1 kilogram because *kilo* means "1,000."

MAKE MEASUREMENTS

Weight/Force

You use a spring scale to measure weight. An object has weight because the force of gravity pulls down on the object. Therefore, weight is a force. Like all forces weight is measured in newtons (N).

Measure the Weight of an Object

1. Look at your spring scale to see how many newtons it measures. See how the measurements are divided. The spring scale shown here measures up to 10 N. It has a mark for every 1 N.
2. Hold the spring scale by the top loop. Put the object to be measured on the bottom hook. If the object will not stay on the hook, place it in a net bag. Then hang the bag from the hook.
3. Let go of the object slowly. It will pull down on a spring inside the scale. The spring is connected to a pointer. The pointer on the spring scale shown here is a small arrow.
4. Wait for the pointer to stop moving. Read the number of newtons next to the pointer. This is the object's weight. The mug in the picture weighs 3 N.

More About Spring Scales

You probably weigh yourself by standing on a bathroom scale. This is a spring scale. The force of your body stretches or presses a spring inside the scale. The dial on the scale is probably marked in pounds—the English unit of weight. One pound is equal to about 4.5 newtons.

Here are some spring scales you may have seen.

R16

Temperature

Temperature is how hot or cold something is. You use a thermometer to measure temperature. A thermometer is made of a thin tube with colored liquid inside. When the liquid gets warmer, it expands and moves up the tube. When the liquid gets cooler, it contracts and moves down the tube. You may have seen most temperatures measured in degrees Fahrenheit (°F). Scientists measure temperature in degrees Celsius (°C).

Read a Thermometer

1. Look at the thermometer shown here. It has two scales—a Fahrenheit scale and a Celsius scale. Every 20 degrees on each scale has a number.
2. What is the temperature shown on the thermometer? At what temperature does water freeze? Give your answers in °F and in °C.

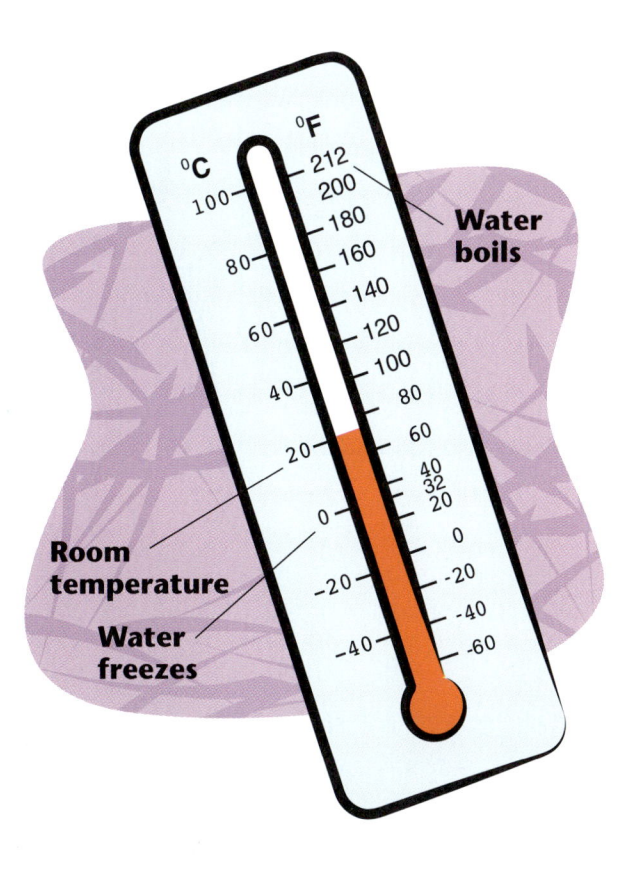

How Is Temperature Measured?

1. Fill a large beaker about one-half full of cool water. Find the temperature of the water by holding a thermometer in the water. Do not let the bulb at the bottom of the thermometer touch the sides or bottom of the beaker.
2. Keep the thermometer in the water until the liquid in the tube stops moving—about a minute. Read and record the temperature on the Celsius scale.
3. Fill another large beaker one-half full of warm water from a faucet. Be careful not to burn yourself by using hot water.
4. Find and record the temperature of the warm water just as you did in steps 1 and 2.

MAKE OBSERVATIONS

Weather

What was the weather like yesterday? What is it like today? The weather changes from day to day. You can observe different parts of the weather to find out how it changes.

Measure Temperature

1. Use a thermometer to find the air temperature outside. Look at page R17 to review thermometers.
2. Hold a thermometer outside for two minutes. Then read and record the temperature.
3. Take the temperature at the same time each day for a week. Record it in a chart.

Clear skies; no clouds   **Partly cloudy**   **Cloudy**

2. Record in your chart if it is raining or snowing.
3. At the end of the week, how has the weather changed from day to day?

Observe Wind Speed and Direction

1. Observe how the wind is affecting things around you. Look at a flag or the branches of a tree. How hard is the wind blowing the flag or branches? Observe for about five minutes. Write down your observations.
2. Hold a compass to see which direction the wind is coming from. Write down this direction.
3. Observe the wind each day for a week. Record your observations in your chart.

Observe Clouds, Rain, and Snow

1. Observe how much of the sky is covered by clouds. Use these symbols to record the cloud cover in your chart each day.

MONDAY
25°C
Strong winds from south
● Rain

TUESDAY
23°C
Light wind

WEDNESDAY

R18

Systems

What do a toy car, a tomato plant, and a yo-yo have in common? They are all systems. A system is a set of parts that work together to form a whole. Look at the three systems below. Think of how each part helps the system work.

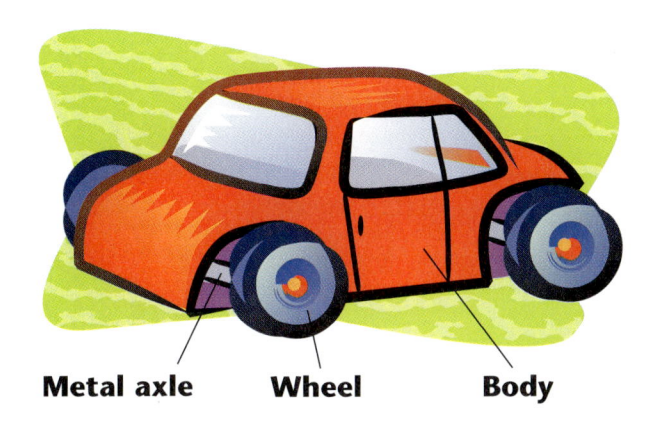

Metal axle   Wheel   Body

This system has three main parts—the body, the axles, and the wheels. Would the system work well if the axles could not turn?

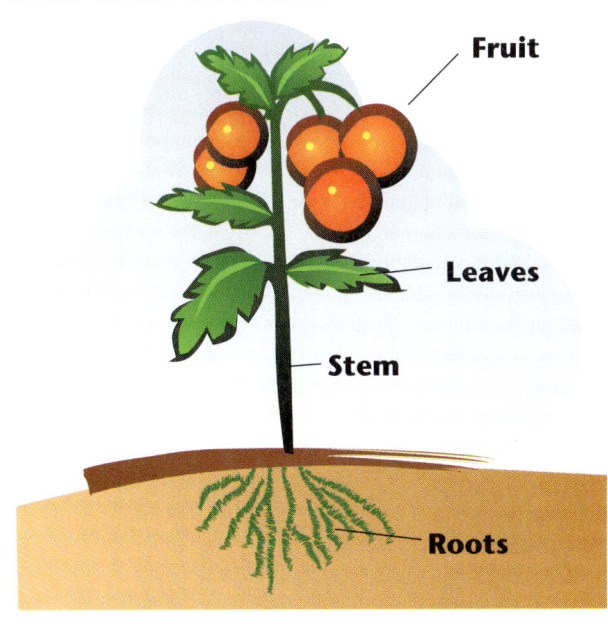

Fruit
Leaves
Stem
Roots

In this system roots take in water, and leaves make food. The stem carries water and food to different parts of the plant. What would happen if you cut off all the leaves?

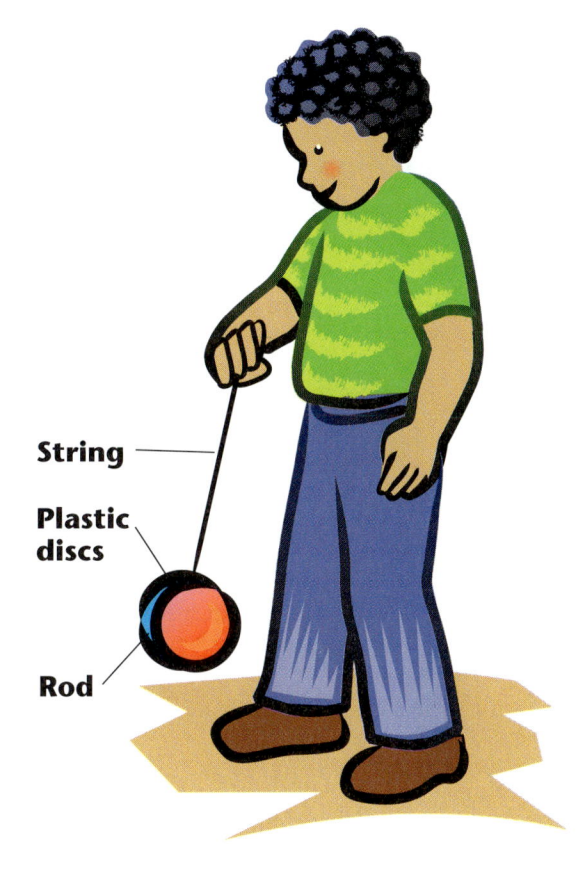

String
Plastic discs
Rod

Even simple things can be systems. How do all the parts of the yo-yo work together to make the toy go up and down?

Look for some other systems at school, at home, and outside. Remember to look for things that are made of parts. List the parts. Then describe how you think each part helps the system work.

R19

REPRESENT DATA

Make Graphs to Organize Data

When you do an experiment in science, you collect information. To find out what your information means, you can organize it into graphs. There are many kinds of graphs.

Bar Graphs

A bar graph uses bars to show information. For example, suppose you are growing a plant. Every week you measure how high the plant has grown. Here is what you find.

Week	Height (cm)
1	1
2	3
3	6
4	10
5	17
6	20
7	22
8	23

The bar graph at right organizes the measurements you collected so that you can easily compare them.

1. Look at the bar for week 2. Put your finger at the top of the bar. Move your finger straight over to the left to find how many centimeters the plant grew by the end of week 2.
2. Between which two weeks did the plant grow most?
3. When did plant growth begin to level off?

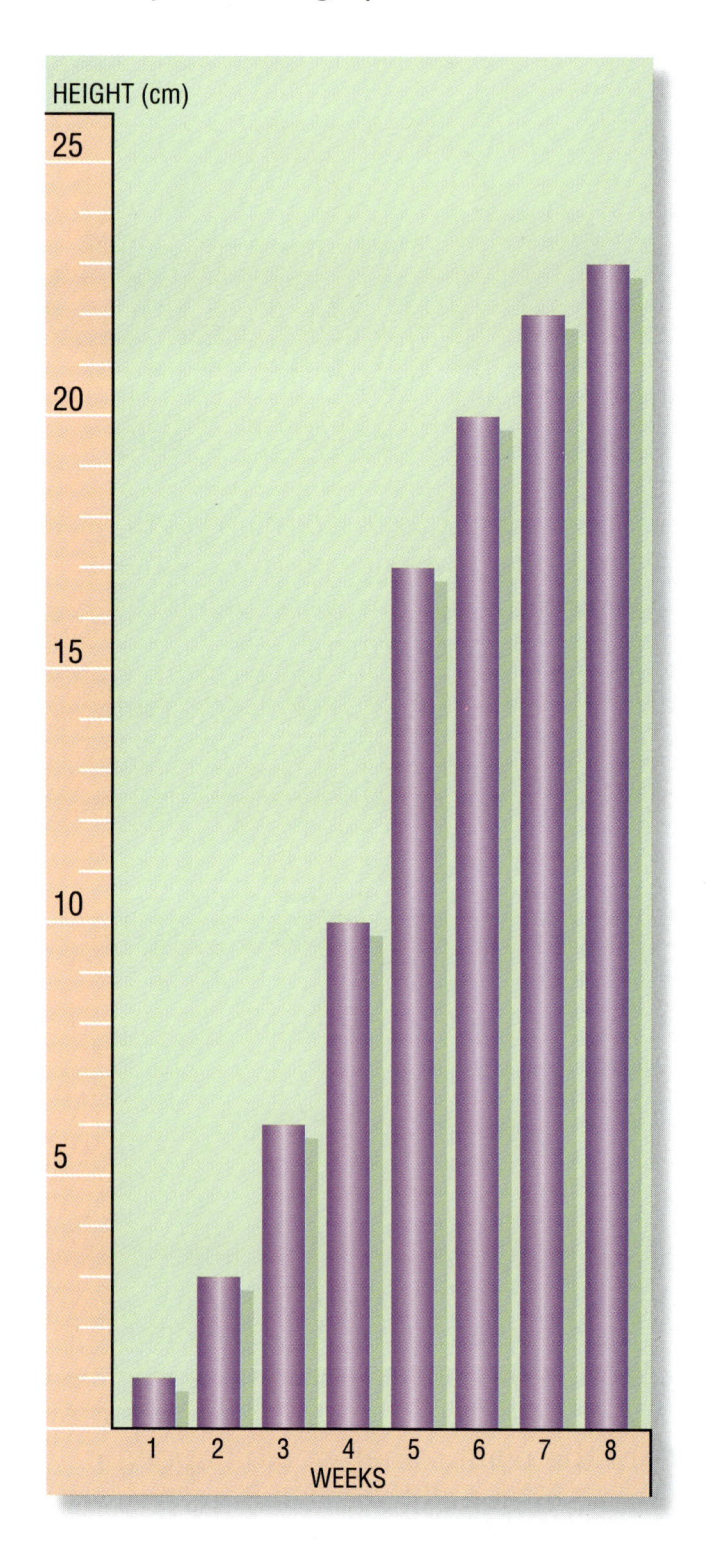

Pictographs

A pictograph uses symbols, or pictures, to show information. Suppose you collect information about how much water your family uses each day. Here is what you find.

Activity	Water Used Each Day (L)
Drinking	10
Showering	180
Bathing	240
Brushing teeth	80
Washing dishes	140
Washing hands	30
Washing clothes	280
Flushing toilet	90

You can organize this information into the pictograph shown here. The pictograph has to explain what the symbol on the graph means. In this case, each bottle means 20 liters of water. A half bottle means half of 20, or 10 liters of water.

1. Which activity uses the most water?
2. Which activity uses the least water?

Make a Graph

Suppose you do an experiment to find out how far a toy car rolls on different surfaces. The results of your experiment are shown below.

Surface	Distance Car Rolled (cm)
Wood Floor	525
Sidewalk	325
Carpet Floor	150
Tile Floor	560
Grass	55

1. Decide what kind of graph would best show these results.
2. Make your graph.

A Family's Daily Use of Water

= 20 liters of water

REPRESENT DATA

Make Maps to Show Information

Locate Places MATH LINK

A map is a drawing that shows an area from above. Most maps have numbers and letters along the top and side. They help you find places easily. For example, what if you wanted to find the library on the map below. It is located at D7. Place a finger on the letter D along the side of the map and another finger on the number 7 at the top. Then move your fingers straight across and down the map until they meet. The library is located where D and 7 meet, or very nearby.

1. What building is located at G3?
2. The hospital is located three blocks south and three blocks east of the library. What is its number and letter?
3. Make a map of an area in your community. It might be a park or the area between your home and school. Include numbers and letters along the top and side. Use a compass to find north, and mark north on your map. Exchange maps with classmates.

Idea Maps

The map below left shows how places are connected to each other. Idea maps, on the other hand, show how ideas are connected to each other. Idea maps help you organize information about a topic.

Look at the idea map below. It connects ideas about water. This map shows that Earth's water is either fresh water or salt water. The map also shows four sources of fresh water. You can see that there is no connection between "rivers" and "salt water" on the map. This reminds you that salt water does not flow in rivers.

Make an idea map about a topic you are learning in science. Your map can include words, phrases, or even sentences. Arrange your map in a way that makes sense to you and helps you understand the ideas.

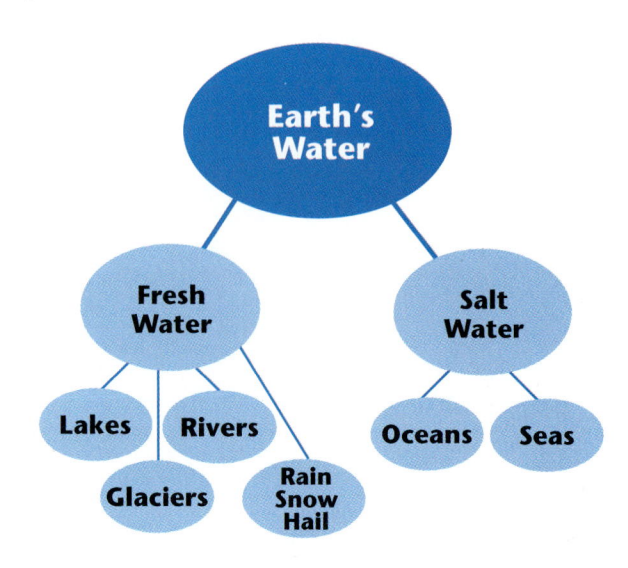

Make Tables and Charts to Organize Data

Tables help you organize data during experiments. Most tables have columns that run up and down, and rows that run across. The columns and rows have headings that tell you what kind of data goes in each part of the table.

A Sample Table

What if you are going to do an experiment to find out how long different kinds of seeds take to sprout? Before you begin the experiment, you should set up your table. Follow these steps.

1. In this experiment you will plant 20 radish seeds, 20 bean seeds, and 20 corn seeds. Your table must show how many of each kind of seed sprouted on days 1, 2, 3, 4, and 5.
2. Make your table with columns, rows, and headings. You might use a computer. Some computer programs let you build a table with just the click of a mouse. You can delete or add columns and rows if you need to.
3. Give your table a title. Your table could look like the one here.

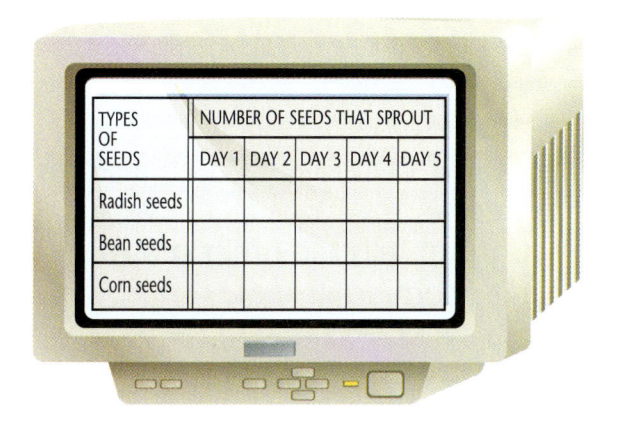

TYPES OF SEEDS	NUMBER OF SEEDS THAT SPROUT				
	DAY 1	DAY 2	DAY 3	DAY 4	DAY 5
Radish seeds					
Bean seeds					
Corn seeds					

Make a Table

Now what if you are going to do an experiment to find out how temperature affects the sprouting of seeds? You will plant 20 bean seeds in each of two trays. You will keep each tray at a different temperature, as shown below, and observe the trays for seven days. Make a table that you can use for this experiment. You can use the table to record, examine, and evaluate the information of this experiment

Make a Chart

A chart is simply a table with pictures as well as words to label the rows or columns. Make a chart that shows the information of the experiment above.

R23

USE TECHNOLOGY

Computer

A computer has many uses. The Internet connects your computer to many other computers around the world, so you can collect all kinds of information. You can use a computer to show this information and write reports. Best of all you can use a computer to explore, discover, and learn.

You can also get information from CD-ROMs. They are computer disks that can hold large amounts of information. You can fit a whole encyclopedia on one CD-ROM.

Use Computers for a Project

Here is how one group of students uses computers as they work on a weather project.

1. The students use instruments to measure temperature, wind speed, wind direction, and other parts of the weather. They input this information, or data, into the computer. The students keep the data in a table. This helps them compare the data from one day to the next.

2. The teacher finds out that another group of students in a town 200 kilometers to the west is also doing a weather project. The two groups use the Internet to talk to each other and share data. When a storm happens in the town to the west, that group tells the other group that it's coming its way.

email: It's going to storm here. The sky is turning dark gray. The winds are sometimes 65 km per hour from the northwest.

3. The students want to find out more. They decide to stay on the Internet and send questions to a local TV weather forecaster. She has a Web site and answers questions from students every day.

4. Meanwhile some students go to the library to gather more information from a CD-ROM disk. The CD-ROM has an encyclopedia that includes movie clips with sound. The clips give examples of different kinds of storms.

5. The students have kept all their information in a folder called Weather Project. Now they use that information to write a report about the weather. On the computer they can move paragraphs, add words, take out words, put in diagrams, and draw their own weather maps. Then they print the report in color.

6. Use the information on these two pages to plan your own investigation. You can study the weather, use a computer, Internet, CD-ROM, or any technological device.

USE TECHNOLOGY

Calculator

Sometimes after you make measurements, you have to add or subtract your numbers. A calculator helps you do this.

Add and Subtract Rainfall Amounts

The table shows the amount of rain that fell in a town each week during the summer. The amounts are given in centimeters (cm). Use a calculator to find the total amount of rain that fell during the summer.

Week	Rain (cm)
1	3
2	5
3	2
4	0
5	1
6	6
7	4
8	0
9	2
10	2
11	6
12	5

1. Make sure the calculator is on. Press the ON key.
2. To add the numbers, enter a number and press +. Repeat until you enter the last number. Then press =. You do not have to enter the zeroes. Your total should be 36.
3. Suppose you found out that you made a mistake in your measurements. Week 1 should be 2 cm less, Week 6 should be 3 cm less, Week 11 should be 1 cm less, and Week 12 should be 2 cm less. Subtract these numbers from your total. You should have 36 displayed on the calculator. Press − and enter the first number you want to subtract. Repeat until you enter the last number. Then press =. Compare your new total to your classmates' new totals.

GLOSSARY

This Glossary will help you to pronounce and understand the meanings of the Science Words introduced in this book. The page number at the end of the definition tells where the word appears.

A

adaptation (ad′əp tā′shən) A characteristic that helps an organism survive in its environment. (p. 364)

antibody (an′ti bod′ē) A chemical made by the immune system to fight a particular disease. (p. 401)

asteroid (as′tə roid′) A small chunk of rock or metal that orbits the Sun. (p. 250)

atom (at′əm) The smallest particle of matter. (p. 157)

atmosphere (at′məs fîr′) A layer of gases surrounding a planet. (p. 238)

axis (ak′sis) A real or imaginary line through the center of a spinning object. (p. 197)

B

bacteria (bak tîr′ē ə) One-celled living things. (p. 399)

PRONUNCIATION KEY

a	at	e	end	o	hot	u	up	hw	white	ə	about
ā	ape	ē	me	ō	old	ū	use	ng	song		taken
ä	far	i	it	ô	fork	ü	rule	th	thin		pencil
âr	care	ī	ice	oi	oil	u̇	pull	<u>th</u>	this		lemon
		îr	pierce	ou	out	ûr	turn	zh	measure		circus

′ = primary accent; shows which syllable takes the main stress, such as **kil** in **kilogram** (kil′ə gram′)
′ = secondary accent; shows which syllables take lighter stresses, such as **gram** in **kilogram**

R27

camouflage • conifer

camouflage (kam′ə fläzh′) An adaptation that allows organisms to blend into their surroundings. (p. 366)

carbohydrate (kär′bō hī′drāt) A substance used by the body as its main source of energy. (p. 412)

carbon dioxide and oxygen cycle (kär′bən dī ok′sīd and ok′sə jən sī′kəl) The exchange of gases between producers and consumers. (p. 344)

cell (sel) 1. Tiny box-like part that is the basic building block of living things. (p. 56) 2. A source of electricity. (p. 184)

cell membrane (sel mem′brān) A thin outer covering of plant and animal cells. (p. 57)

circuit (sûr′kit) The path electricity flows through. (p. 184)

comet (kom′it) A body of ice and rock that orbits the Sun. (p. 250)

communicate (kə mū′ni kāt′) To share information by sending, receiving, and responding to signals. (p. 8)

community (kə mū′ni tē) All the living things in an ecosystem. (p. 324)

competition (kom′pi tish′ən) When one organism works against another to get what it needs to live. (p. 356)

compound (kom′pound) Two or more elements put together. (p. 158)

compound machine (kom′pound mə shēn′) Two or more simple machines put together. (p. 122)

conifer (kon′ə fər) A tree that produces seeds inside of cones. (p. 35)

GLOSSARY

consumer (kən sü′mər) An organism that eats producers or other consumers. (p. 334)

corona (kə rō′nə) The outermost layer of gases surrounding the Sun. (p. 229)

crater (krā′tər) A hollow area in the ground. (p. 208)

cytoplasm (sī′tə plaz′əm) A clear, jelly-like material that fills plant and animal cells. (p. 57)

D

data (dā′tə) Information. (p. 82)

decomposer (dē′kəm pō′zər) An organism that breaks down dead plant and animal material. (p. 336)

degree (di grē′) The unit of measurement for temperature. (p. 166)

dermis (dûr′mis) The layer of skin just below the epidermis. (p. 390)

development (di vel′əp mənt) The way a living thing changes during its life. (p. 4)

digestion (di jes′chən) The process of breaking down food. (p. 422)

E

earthquake (ûrth′kwāk′) A sudden movement in the rocks that make up Earth's crust. (p. 282)

eclipse (i klips′) When one object passes into the shadow of another object. (p. 218)

ecosystem (ek′ō sis′təm) All the living and nonliving things in an environment. (p. 324)

element (el′ə mənt) A building block of matter. (p. 157)

PRONUNCIATION KEY

a at; ā ape; ä far; âr care; e end; ē me; i it; ī ice; îr pierce; o hot; ō old; ô fork; oi oil; ou out; u up; ū use; ü rule; u̇ pull; ûr turn; hw white; ng song; th thin; <u>th</u> this; zh measure; ə about, taken, pencil, lemon, circus

electric current (i lek′trik kûr′ənt) Electricity that flows through a circuit. (p. 184)

embryo (em′brē ō) A young organism that is just beginning to grow. (p. 34)

endangered (en dān′jərd) In danger of becoming extinct. (p. 378)

energy (en′ər jē) The ability to do work. (p. 14, 101)

energy pyramid (en′ər jē pir′ə mid′) A diagram that shows how energy is used in an ecosystem. (p. 339)

environment (en vī′rən mənt) The things that make up an area, such as the land, water, and air. (p. 6)

epidermis (ep′ə dûr′mis) The outer layer of skin. (p. 388)

erosion (i rō′zhən) The process that occurs when weathered materials are carried away. (p. 272)

extinct (ek stingkt′) When there are no more of a certain plant or animal. (p. 378)

F

fats (fatz) Substances used by the body as long-lasting sources of energy. (p. 413)

fertilizer (fûr′tə lī′zər) A substance used to keep plants healthy. (p. 311)

fiber (fī′bər) Material that helps move wastes through the body. (p. 414)

flowering plant (flou′ər ing plant) A plant that produces seeds inside of flowers. (p. 35)

food chain (füd chān) A series of organisms that depend on one another for food. (p. 334)

food web (füd web) Several food chains that are connected. (p. 338)

force (fôrs) A push or pull. (p. 78)

friction (frik′shən) A force that occurs when one object rubs against another. (p. 90)

fuel (fū′əl) Something burned to provide heat or power. (p. 230)

G

gas (gas) Matter that has no definite shape or volume. (p. 142)

germinate (jûr′mə nāt) To begin growing. (p. 34)

glacier (glā′shər) A large mass of ice in motion. (p. 272)

gland (gland) A part of the body that makes substances the body needs. (p. 389)

gravity (grav′i tē) The pulling force between two objects. (p. 80)

H

habitat (hab′i tat′) The place where a plant or animal naturally lives and grows. (p. 324)

heat (hēt) A form of energy that makes things warmer. (p. 166)

helper T-cells (hel′pər tē selz) White blood cells that send signals to warn that germs have invaded the body. (p. 401)

hibernate (hī′bər nāt′) To rest or sleep through the cold winter. (p. 18)

host (hōst) The organism a parasite lives in or on. (p. 347)

hurricane (hûr′i kān′) A violent storm with strong winds and heavy rains. (p. 280)

PRONUNCIATION KEY

a at; ā ape; ä far; âr care; e end; ē me; i it; ī ice; îr pierce; o hot; ō old; ô fork; oi oil; ou out; u up; ū use; ü rule; u̇ pull; ûr turn; hw white; ng song; th thin; <u>th</u> this; zh measure; ə about, taken, pencil, lemon, circus

GLOSSARY

I

immune system (i mūn′ sis′təm) All the body parts and activities that fight diseases. (p. 403)

immunity (i mū′ni tē) The body's ability to fight diseases caused by germs. (p. 403)

inclined plane (in klīnd′ plān) A flat surface that is raised at one end. (p. 118)

inherited trait (in her′i təd trāt) A characteristic that comes from your parents. (p. 28)

insulator (in′sə lā′tər) A material that heat doesn't travel through easily. (p. 170)

L

landform (land′fôrm′) A feature on the surface of Earth. (p. 264)

large intestine (lärj in tes′tin) Part of the body that removes water from undigested food. (p. 425)

learned trait (lûrnd trāt) Something that you are taught or learn from experience. (p. 28)

lens (lenz) A curved piece of glass. (p. 240)

lever (lev′ər) A straight bar that moves on a fixed point. (p. 109)

life cycle (līf sī′kəl) All the stages in an organism's life. (p. 24)

liquid (lik′wid) Matter that has a definite volume, but not a definite shape. (p. 142)

lunar eclipse (lü′nər i klips′) When Earth's shadow blocks the Moon. (p. 219)

M

machine (mə shēn′) A tool that makes work easier to do. (p. 108)

magnetism (mag′ni tiz′əm) The property of an object that makes it attract iron. (p. 154)

mass (mas) How much matter is in an object. (p. 133)

matter (mat′ər) What makes up an object. (p. 80)

melanin (mel′ə nin) A substance that gives skin its color. (p. 388)

metal (met′əl) A shiny material found in the ground. (p. 154)

metamorphosis (met′ə môr′fə sis) A change in the body form of an organism. (p. 25)

migrate (mī′grāt) To move to another place. (p. 18)

mineral (min′ə rəl) A substance found in nature that is not a plant or an animal. (pp. 49, 260)

mixture (miks′chər) Different types of matter mixed together. (p. 147)

motion (mō′shən) A change of position. (p. 70)

N

natural resource (nach′ər əl rē′sôrs′) A material on Earth that is necessary or useful to people. (p. 292)

nerve cells (nûrv selz) Cells that carry messages to and from all parts of the body. (p. 390)

newton (nü′tən) The unit used to measure pushes and pulls. (p. 78)

niche (nich) The job or role an organism has in an ecosystem. (p. 358)

PRONUNCIATION KEY

a **at**; ā **ape**; ä **far**; âr **care**; e **end**; ē **me**; i **it**; ī **ice**; îr **pierce**; o **hot**; ō **old**; ô **fork**; oi **oil**; ou **out**; u **up**; ū **use**; ü **rule**; ů **pull**; ûr **turn**; hw **white**; ng **song**; th **thin**; <u>th</u> **this**; zh **measure**; ə **about, taken, pencil, lemon, circus**

GLOSSARY

nonrenewable resource • plateau

nonrenewable resource (non′ri nü′ə bəl rē′sôrs′) A resource that cannot be reused or replaced in a useful amount of time. (p. 302)

nucleus (nü′klē əs) A main control center found in plant and animal cells. (p. 57)

nutrient (nüt′rē ənt) A substance that your body needs for energy and growth. (p. 412)

O

opaque (ō pāk′) Does not allow light to pass through. (p. 176)

orbit (ôr′bit) The path an object follows as it revolves. (p. 198)

organ (ôr′gən) A group of tissues that work together. (p. 58)

organism (ôr′gə niz′əm) A living thing. (p. 4)

oxygen (ok′sə jən) A gas that is in air and water. (p. 16)

P

parasite (par′ə sīt) An organism that lives in or on another organism. (p. 347)

perish (per′ish) To not survive. (p. 377)

phase (fāz) Apparent change in the Moon's shape. (p. 207)

plain (plān) A large area of land with few hills. (p. 264)

planet (plan′it) A satellite of the Sun. (p. 228)

plateau (pla tō′) A flat area of land that rises above the land that surrounds it. (p. 265)

pollution (pə lü′shən) What happens when harmful substances get into water, air, or land. (p. 310)

population (pop′yə lā′shən) All the members of a certain type of living thing in an area. (p. 324)

pore (pôr) A tiny opening in the skin. (p. 391)

position (pə zish′ən) The location of an object. (p. 68)

pound (pound) The unit used to measure force and weight in the English system of measurement. (p. 81)

predator (pred′ə tər) An animal that hunts other animals for food. (p. 356)

prey (prā) The animal a predator hunts. (p. 356)

producer (prə dü′sər) An organism that makes its own food. (p. 334)

property (prop′ər tē) A characteristic of something. (p. 135)

protein (prō′tēn) A substance that the body uses for growth and the repair of cells. (p. 413)

pulley (pul′ē) A simple machine that uses a wheel and a rope. (p. 112)

R

recycle (rē sī′kəl) To treat something so it can be used again. (p. 314)

reduce (ri düs′) To make less of something. (p. 312)

reflect (ri flekt′) To bounce off a surface. (p. 177)

relocate (ri lō′kāt) To find a new home. (p. 377)

PRONUNCIATION KEY

a **at**; ā **ape**; ä **far**; âr **care**; e **end**; ē **me**; i **it**; ī **ice**; îr **pierce**; o **hot**; ō **old**; ô **fork**; oi **oil**; ou **out**; u **up**; ū **use**; ü **rule**; u̇ **pull**; ûr **turn**; hw **white**; ng **song**; th **thin**; <u>th</u> **this**; zh measure; ə about, taken, pencil, lemon, circus

renewable resource • solid

renewable resource (ri nü′ə bəl rē′sôrs′) A resource that can be replaced or used over and over again. (p. 296)

reproduction (rē′prə duk′shən) The way organisms make new living things just like themselves. (p. 5)

respond (ri spond′) The way a living thing reacts to changes in its environment. (p. 6)

reuse (v., rē ūz′) To use something again. (p. 314)

revolve (ri volv′) To move in a circle around an object. (p. 198)

rotate (rō′tāt) To turn around. (p. 196)

S

saliva (sə lī′və) A liquid in your mouth that helps soften and break down food. (p. 423)

satellite (sat′ə līt′) An object that orbits another, larger object in space. (p. 206)

screw (skrü) An inclined plane wrapped into a spiral. (p. 120)

simple machine (sim′pəl mə shēn′) A machine with few or no moving parts. (p. 109)

small intestine (smôl in tes′tin) A tube-like part of your body where most digestion takes place. (p. 425)

solar eclipse (sō′lər i klips′) When the Moon's shadow blocks the Sun. (p. 218)

solar system (sō′lər sis′təm) The Sun and all the objects that orbit the Sun. (p. 236)

solid (sol′id) Matter that has a definite shape and volume. (p. 142)

solution (sə lü′shən) A type of mixture that has one or more types of matter spread evenly through another. (p. 148)

speed (spēd) How fast an object moves. (p. 71)

star (stär) A hot sphere of gases that gives off energy. (p. 228)

stomach (stum′ək) Part of your body that has walls made of strong muscles that squeeze and mash food. (p. 424)

sunspot (sun′spot′) A dark area on the Sun's surface. (p. 229)

switch (swich) Opens or closes an electric circuit. (p. 185)

system (sis′təm) A group of parts that work together. (p. 46)

T

taste buds (tāst budz) Thousands of cells on your tongue that send the signals for sweet, sour, bitter, and salty to your brain. (p. 423)

telescope (tel′ə skōp′) A tool that gathers light to make faraway objects appear closer. (p. 240)

temperature (tem′pər ə chər) A measure of how hot or cold something is. (p. 166)

tissue (tish′ü) A group of cells that are alike. (p. 58)

V

vaccine (vak′sēn) A medicine that causes the body to form antibodies against a certain disease. (p. 404)

valley (val′ē) An area of land lying between hills. (p. 264)

PRONUNCIATION KEY

a at; ā ape; ä far; âr care; e end; ē me; i it; ī ice; îr pierce; o hot; ō old; ô fork; oi oil; ou out; u up; ū use; ü rule; ü pull; ûr turn; hw white; ng song; th thin; th this; zh measure; ə about, taken, pencil, lemon, circus

GLOSSARY

virus • work

virus (vī′rəs) A tiny particle that can reproduce only inside a living cell. (p. 399)

vitamin (vīt′ə mən) A substance used by the body for growth. (p. 414)

volcano (vol kā′nō) An opening in the surface of Earth. Melted rock, gases, rock pieces, and dust are forced out of this opening. (p. 283)

volume (vol′ūm) How much space matter takes up. (p. 132)

W

weathering (we<u>th</u>′ər ing) The process that causes rocks to crumble, crack, and break. (p. 270)

wedge (wej) Two inclined planes placed back to back. (p. 119)

weight (wāt) The pull of gravity on an object. (p. 81)

wheel and axle (hwēl and ak′səl) A wheel that turns on a post. (p. 111)

white blood cells (hwīt blud selz) Cells in the blood that fight bacteria and viruses. (p. 400)

work (würk) When a force changes the motion of an object. (p. 100)

INDEX

A

Adaptation, 364–366, 368, 381
AIDS, 406–407
Air, 16, 210, 305
Aluminum, 156–157
Animals, 22-23*, 24–27, 28*–29, 46-50*, 51, 57, 323*, 330-331, 334, 342–343*, 344-348*, 349, 356–359, 362–363*, 364, 374–378*
Antibodies, 401–402*, 404, 408
Area, R2–R3, R11
Asteroids, 250, 253
Atmosphere, 238–239, 253
Atom, 152, 157, 161–162
Ax, 119
Axis, 197–198, 201, 224, 236, 256
Axles, 111, 113, 125

B

Bacteria, 336, 399, 408, 426
Balance, R14–R15, R20–21
Bar graph, 82*, 304*
Basalt, 262
Bear, 26
Biceps, 84–85
Bird, 27
Birth, 24–27
Blood, 391
Body parts, 44–45*, 46–50*, 51, 54–55*, 56*-59
Body system, 58
Body temperature, 391
Bulbs, 38

C

Calculator, R26
Calendar, 212–213
Camera, R10
Camouflage, 366–367*, 381
Carbohydrates, 412, 429
Carbon dioxide, 210, 239, 344–345
Carbon dioxide and oxygen cycle, 344–345, 352
Carver, George Washington, 298–299
Cell, electrical, 183*–184, 189, 192
Cell membrane, 57, 61
Cells, 56*, 57–59, 61
Cellulose, 60
Cell wall, 57
Celsius scale, R2–R3, R17
Centimeter, R2–R3
Chalk, changing, 271*
Changes
    in ecosystems, 372–373*,374–378*, 379
    in living things, 3*–4, 22–23*, 24–27, 28*–29
    in matter, 144–145, 150–151, 168–169*, 177
    in motion, 87*–89, 100
    in rocks, 269*–270
Charts, reading, 27, 71, 143, 177, 184, 313, 357, 364, 368, 416, R23
Chemicals, 270–271*
Chlorine, 158
Chloroplasts, 57
Circuits, 184–185*, 189

Classifying, 50*, 61, 63, 141*–142, 146
Cleaning water, 311*
Clock, R12
Closed circuit, 184
Coal, 230, 302–303
Comets, 250, 253
Communicating, 8, 42, 146*, 191
Community, 324, 328*, 350–352
Comparing the Sun and Moon, 231*
Compass, R8, R10
Competition, 354–355*, 356–358*, 359, 361, 381
Compost, 39
Compound machines, 122–123, 125
Compounds, 158–159, 162
Computer, R24–R25
Conglomerate, 262
Conifers, 35–36, 42
Conservation, 188, 308–309*, 310–311*, 312–315, 360-361
Consumers, 334, 337*, 344–345, 352
Contour farming, 266–267
Contraction, 169
Controlling electrical flow, 185
Controlling experiments, 178*
Copper, 156–157
Corona, 229, 231, 253
Craters, 208, 210, 224, 239
Cuttings, 38
Cytoplasm, 57, 61

* Indicates an activity related to this topic.

R39

Day – Evaporation

D

Day, 194–195*, 196
Death, 24
Decomposers, 336–337*, 352
Defining terms, 328*
Degrees, 166, 189, R2–R3
Dermis, 390–391, 408
Desert, 52, 322, 335, 356, 368
Designing experiments, 45*, 63, 107*, 127, 141*, 191, 245*, 255, 279*, 319, 363*, 383, 387*, 431
Development, 4, 9, 24, 26–27, 36
Diagrams, reading, 4, 16, 35, 57, 70, 72, 79, 88, 102, 109, 136, 167, 189, 199, 206, 219, 230, 237, 263, 271, 283, 303, 325, 327, 335, 376, 389, 401, 423
Digestion, 409, 422*–427, 429
Digestive system, 426–427, 432
Disease, 381, 388–389, 396–397*, 398–402*, 403–405
Distance, 67*, 71, 217*, R2–R3
Dust bowl, 284

E

Earth, 104–105, 194–195*, 196–200*, 201, 206–211, 214–215*, 216–222, 227*–228, 234–235*, 236–241, 258–259*, 260–261*, 262–265, 268–269*, 270–271*, 272–273*, 274–275, 278–279*, 280, 282–285, 290–291*, 292–295*, 296–297
Earthquakes, 104–105, 282–283
Earth's surface, 264–265, 268–269*, 270–271*, 272–273*, 274–275, 278–279*, 280–281*, 282–285, 290–291*, 292–294, 296–297
  changes to, 268–269*, 278–279*, 280–281*, 282–283
Eclipse, 218–224
Ecosystems, 323*, 324–327, 328*–331, 336–337*, 338–339, 343*–344, 357, 358*–359, 368, 372–373*, 374–377, 378*–379
Eggs, 30–31
Electric current, 173, 182–187, 189
Electrical flow, 185*
Electricity, 182–183*, 184–185*, 186–189, 192
Elements, 157–159, 160–162
Embryo, 34, 42
Endangered species, 378*–379, 381
Energy, 14, 16, 42, 49, 101*–102, 104–105, 143, 145, 166, 168, 171, 172–173, 176–177, 180–181, 226–227*, 229–230, 233, 302, 304*, 336, 360–361, 412
  from the Sun, 180–181
Energy, stored, 12, 101–102, 104–105, 173, 176, 226–227
  in batteries, 101, 182–187, 233
  conversion to heat, 104–105, 168, 171, 226–227, 230, 233, 336, 360–361
  conversion to motion, 14, 24, 49, 88–89, 98, 101–113, 171, 182–187, 230, 233, 334, 339, 360–361
  in food, 14, 24, 230, 233, 334, 340–341
  in fuel, 101, 171, 230, 233, 340–341
Energy pyramid, 339
Energy survey, 304*
Energy transformation, 336
English system of measures, R2–R3
Environment, 6–7*, 8–9, 18, 19, 48, 274, 322–323*, 324–328*, 362–363*, 364–367*, 368–369
  changes to, caused by living things
    beneficial, 35, 324–325, 336–337, 344–345
    detrimental, 30–31, 40–41, 346–349, 380
  response of plants and animals to changes in, 6–8, 18, 20–21, 30–31, 168, 372–380
Epidermis, 389, 390, 397*, 408
Epiglottis, 428
Equal forces, 89
Erosion, 266–267, 272, 273*, 274–279*, 280–281*, 296
Esophagus, 424
Evaporation, 145, 148, 172–173

R40   * Indicates an activity related to this topic.

INDEX

Expansion, 169
Experimenting, 7*
Experiments, 7*, 45*, 63, 64, 107*, 127, 141*, 178*, 191, 245*, 255, 279*, 319, 383, 387*, 431. *See also* Explore activities *and* Quick Labs.
Explore activities, 3*, 13*, 23*, 33*, 45*, 55*, 67*, 77*, 87*, 99*, 107*, 117*, 131*, 141*, 153*, 165*, 175*, 183*, 195*, 205*, 215*, 227*, 235*, 245*, 259*, 279*, 291*, 301*, 309*, 311*, 323*, 333*, 343*, 355*, 373*, 387*, 397*, 411*, 421*
Extinction, 378*–379, 381

F

Fahrenheit scale, R2–R3, R17
Fats, 411*– 413, 429
Fertilizers, 311
Fiber, 414, 429
Flashlight, 185*
Flowering plants, 35, 42
Food, 332–333*, 340–341, 344–345, 410–411*, 412–415*, 416–417, 418–419, 420–421*, 422*–428
Food chains, 334–335, 338, 352
Food pyramid, 416
Food webs, 338, 352
Forces, 77*–81, 86–87*, 88–92*, 93, 94, 100, 109–110, 112, 119, R3, R16
Forest, 325, 328, 357–359, 376
Forest community, 328*

Forming a hypothesis, 273*
Formulating a model, 402*
Fortified cereal, 155*
Freeze-dried foods, 418–419
Friction, 90–91, 92*, 93, 94–95, 102, 104–105, 171
Frog, 25, 30–31
Fuels, 230, 233, 253, 302
Fulcrum, 109–110*
Fungi, 336

G

Gases, 16, 49, 142–143, 145–146*, 147–149, 150–151, 157, 169*, 210, 230–231, 248, 249, 250, 283, 302, 305, 344–345
Germination, 34, 37, 42
Germs, 396–397*, 398–402*, 403–405, 424, 426
Gills, 16
Glaciers, 272
Gland, 389, 390, 408, 424
Global positioning system, 74–75
Gneiss, 263
Gold, 156–157
Gram, 134, R2–R3
Granite, 260, 263
Graphs, R20–R21
Gravity, 80–81, 82*, 83, 136–137, 210, 220
Great Dark Spot, 249
Great Red Spot, 246
Growth and change, 24–27, 28*, 29

H

Habitat, 324–329, 344–345, 374–378*

Halley's comet, 252
Hand lens, R6
Heat, 164–165*, 166–169*, 170–171, 189, 230, 238
Helper T-cells, 400
Hibernation, 18
HIV virus, 406–407
Homes, 330–331
Host, 347, 352
Hurricanes, 280–281*, 286–289
Hydrogen, 158

I

Ideas, using, 61, 63, 125, 127, 189, 191, 253, 255, 317, 319, 381, 383, 429, 431
Identifying properties, 367*
Immune system, 403–404, 407–408
Immunity, 403, 408
Immunodeficiency, 406–407
Inclined plane, 118, 120, 125
Inferring, 247*, 253, 255
Inherited traits, 28*, 42
Inner planets, 234–235*, 236–237
Insects, 45*–46
Insulators, 170, 189
Interpreting data, 82*, 127*, 415*, 429
Investigating
  ecosystems, 373*
  food, 333*, 411*, 421*
  forces, 77*
  heat, 165*
  light, 175*, 183*
  living things, 3*, 13*, 23*, 55*, 343*
  mining, 301*
  motion, 87*

R41

INDEX

Iron – Matter

night and day, 195*
planets, 235*
plants and animals, 323*, 355*
protection against disease, 397*
rocks, 259*, 269*
shape of the Moon, 205*
size of the Sun and Moon, 215*
soil, 291*
speed, 67*
Sun's energy, 227*
what organisms need, 13*
work, 99*, 117*
Iron, 155*, 158, 187*

J

Journal writing, 63, 127, 191, 255, 319, 383, 431
Jupiter, 83, 236–237, 244–245*, 246–247*

K

Kidneys, 16
Kilogram (kg), 134

L

Landforms, 264, 268, 283
Landslides, 282–283
Large intestine, 425–426, 429
Learned traits, 24, 42
Length, R2–R3, R11
Lenses, 240*
Levers, 109–110*, 113, 114–115, 125, 128
Life cycles, 24–27, 28*–29, 32–33*, 34–37*
Light, 37*, 174–175*, 176–177, 178*–179, 183*–184, 192, 230, 247
and seeing objects, 174–179, 205–209, 218–219, 236, 240, 247
from the Sun, 180–181
Light waves, 180–181
Limestone, 260, 262–263
Liquid, 16, 49, 140–141*, 142–143, 145–146*, 147, 148–149, 150–151, 157, 162, 168, 178*
Lists, identifying, 61, 125
Living things, 2–3*, 4–7*, 8–11, 13*–15*, 16–19, 22–23*, 24–28*, 29, 33*–37*, 38–45*, 46–50*, 51–55*, 56*, 57–61, 322–323*, 324–328*, 329–337, 342–343*, 344–348*, 349–352, 354–355*, 356–358*, 359–363*, 364–369
changes in, 3*–4, 22–23*, 24–27, 28*–29
competition of, 354–355*, 356–358*, 359–361
environment of, 6–7*, 8–9, 18–19, 48, 274, 322–323*, 324–328*, 362–363*, 364–367*, 368–369
features of, 4–5, 6–7*, 8–9
life cycle of, 24–27, 28*–29, 32–33*, 34–37*
needs of, 13*–15*, 16–19, 342–343*, 344–348*, 349
parts of, 44–45*, 46–49, 50*–51, 54–55*, 56*, 57–59
places to live, 322–323*, 324–328*, 329–337
recycling, 336–337
roles for, 342–343*, 344–348*, 349–352
survival of, 362–363*, 364–368*, 369
Length, R2–R3, R11
Lizards, 370–371
Load, 109–110, 112
Lunar calendar, 212–213
Lunar eclipse, 219, 222–224
Lungs, 16

M

Machines, 108–110*, 111–113, 116–117*, 118–121*, 122–125
Magnetism, 154, 162
Magnets, 152–153*, 154
Maps, 72, R10, R22
Marble, 263
Mars, 83, 236–237, 239, 242–243
Mass, 133, 134*, 135–136, 138–139, 210
measuring, 134*, 136, 138–139, 295, R2–R3, R14–R15
Matter, 80–82*, 83, 132–133, 134*–137, 141*–146*, 147–153*, 168–169, 177
building blocks of, 152–153*, 154–155*
changes in, 144–145, 150–151, 168–169*, 177
classifying, 141*–146*
combining, 150–151, 157–159
forms of, 140–141*, 142–143, 147–149
gravity and, 80, 81–82*, 83

R42   * Indicates an activity related to this topic.

Measurement – Organisms

heat and, 164–165*, 166–169*, 170–171, 230, 238
particles of, 133, 142–145, 152, 157, 160–161
properties of, 134*–135, 136–137, 140
Measurement, 134*, 136, 138–139, 295*, R2–R3
Melanin, 388–389, 408
Melting, 145, 160, 167, 169, 172–173
Mercury, 236–237, 238
Metals, 154–155*, 156, 162
Metamorphosis, 25–26, 42
Meters, R2
Metric system, R2–R3
Microscope, 56*, R7
Migration, 18, 42
Millimeter, R2–R3
Minerals, 49, 61, 260–261*, 293, 414
Mineral scratch test, 261
Mining, 301*–302
Mirrors, 174–176
Mixtures, 147–149, 158, 162
Models, making, 402*, 408
Monarch butterfly, 2–21, 24
Moon, 204–205*, 206–208, 209*, 210, 212–213, 214, 215*–216, 217*–222, 231*, 236–23, R9
Motion, 70–73, 86–87*, 88–92*, 93, 94, 99*, 100–101*, 102–103
changes in, 87*–89, 100
defining, 70–71
energy of, 101–102
forces in, 77*–81, 86–87*, 88–92*, 93, 94, 100, 109–110, 112, 119
friction, 90–91, 92*, 93, 94–95, 102, 104–105, 171
of planets, 198, 206–207, 218, 224, 235–238, 239, 246, 248, 249, 250
Movement, 66–67*, 68–73, 86–87*, 88–92*, 93, 99*, 100–101*, 102–103, 235*–236
Moving parts, 46, 48
Moving things, 66–67*, 68–73
position, 68–69*, 70–72
speed, 67*, 71
Muscles, 84–85
Music machines, 114–115

N

Natural gas, 302, 304
Natural resources, 292–297, 300–301*, 302–304*, 305, 360–361
Nectar, 35
Neptune, 236–237, 249
Nerve cells, 390–391, 408
Nerves, 391
Newton, 78, 136, R3
Niche, 358*–359, 381
Night, 194–195*, 196
Nonrenewable resources, 302–303, 360–361
North pole, 197–198
Nucleus, 57, 61
Numbers, using, 121*
Nutrients, 34, 39, 412–415*, 416–417
Nutrition, 409, 415*
Nutrition label, 415

O

Objects, 130–131*, 132–134*, 136–137
Observations, making, 247*, 328*, 367*
Obsidian, 262
Ocean, 331, 334, 345
Oil, 230, 304
Opaque, 176, 189
Open circuit, 184
Orbit, 198, 206–207, 218, 224, 235–238, 239, 246, 248, 249, 250
Organ, 58, 61
Organisms, 4–5, 6–7*, 8–9, 12–13*, 14–19, 22–23*, 24–28*, 29, 44–45*, 46–50*, 51, 54–55*, 56*–59, 323*, 324–327, 328*–331, 336–337*, 338–339, 343*–344, 345–348*, 349, 357, 358*–359, 362–363*, 364–367*, 368–369, 372–373*, 374–377, 378*–379
body parts of, 44–45*, 46–50*, 51, 54–55*, 56*–59
changes in, 3*–4, 22–23*, 24–27, 28*–29
decomposers, 336–337*
ecosystems of, 323*, 324–327, 328*–331, 336–337*, 338–339, 343*–344, 357, 358*–359, 368, 372–373*, 374–377, 378*–379
environment, 322–323*
features of, 3*–7*, 8–9
needs of, 13*–15*, 16–19, 342–343*, 344–348*, 349
organization of, 58

R43

Outer covering – Rocks

response of, 6–7*, 8–9, 17–18, 48
survival characteristics, 362–363*, 364–367*, 368–369, 377–378*
Outer covering, 47
Oxygen, 16, 158, 210, 344–345

P

Parasite, 347, 352
Partial eclipse, 220
Parts of living things, 44–45*, 46–49, 50*–51, 54–55*, 56*–59
  parts of parts, 46
  parts that get information, 46, 48
  parts that move, 46, 48
  parts that protect and support, 46–47, 50*
  parts that take in materials, 46, 49
  smaller, 54–55*, 56*, 57–59
Patterns, using, 209*
Periodic table, 160–161
Perishing, 377–378
Phases, of the Moon, 206–207, 209*, 211, 224
Piano, 114–115
Plain, 264–265
Planetary rings, 246–249
Planets, 228, 234–235*, 236–239, 240*, 241–246, 247*, 248–251, 253
Plant life cycle, 33*–34, 36
Plants, 32–33*, 34–37*, 38–39, 40–41, 46, 52–53, 57, 60, 64, 323*, 330–331, 334, 342–343*, 344–348*, 349, 355*–359, 364–365,

374–375
Plastics, 306–307
Plateau, 265
Plow, 119
Pluto, 236–237, 249
Pollen, 35–36
Pollination, 35–36
Pollution, 308–309*, 310–311*, 312, 316
Pond ecosystem, 326
Population, 324, 344–347, 352
Pores, 391, 408
Position, 68–69*, 70–72
Pounds, 81, R2–R3
Predator, 356, 360–361, 373*, 381
Predicting, 63, 191, 209*, 255
Prey, 356, 373*, 381
Problems and puzzles, 42, 61, 64, 96, 125, 128, 162, 224, 253, 256, 288, 317, 320
Problem solving, 64, 128, 192, 256, 320, 384, 432
Producers, 334, 337*, 344–345, 352
Prominences, 231*
Properties, 135–137, 140–141*, 142–143, 147, 150–151, 153*, 154–155*, 158, 162, 175*, 294, 367*
Proteins, 413
Pulley, 112–113, 125, 128
Pulls, 76–77*, 78–81, 82*, 83, 109
Pushes, 76–77*, 78–81, 82*, 83, 109

Q

Quick Lab, 15*, 28*, 37*, 56*, 69*, 92*, 101*, 110*, 134*, 155*, 169*, 185*, 200*, 217*, 231*, 240*, 261*, 271*, 281*, 337*, 348*, 358*, 378*, 392*, 422*

R

Rabbits, 381
Radar, 288–289
Radiating, 220
Rain forest, 357
Ramp, 117*–118
Rate, R3
Recycling, 314–315, 336–337, R5
Reducing, 312
Reflection, 176–177, 189, 208
Refrigeration, 172–173
Relocation, 377–378
Renewable resources, 296, 300, 305
Reproduction, 5, 9, 24, 33*, 34–36, 38, 42, 348*, 365
Resource conservation, 308–309*, 310–315
Resources, 292–297, 300–301*, 302–304*, 305, 308–309*, 310–315, 360–361
Response of organisms, 6–7*, 8–9, 17–18, 48
Reuse, 314–315
Revolution, 198–199, 210, 224, 236, 239, 248
Rock climbing, 94–95
Rocks, 94–95, 259*–260, 261*–263, 269*, 270, 272–273*, 274–275, 290–291*
  changes in, 269*–270
  comparing, 259*–261*

R44   * Indicates an activity related to this topic.

forming, 262–263
Rotation, 196, 210, 224, 236
Rust, 158

S

Safety rules, R4–R5
Saliva, 423
Sandstone, 262
Satellite, 206, 220, 224, 239
Saturn, 236–237, 248, 256
Schist, 263
Science Journal, 63, 127, 191, 255, 319, 383, 431. *See also* Explore Activities, Quick Lab, Skill Builders.
Screw, 120, 121*, 125
Seasons, 198
Seeds, 35–37*, 348*, 384
Seismic waves, 180–181
Serving size, 415
Shade, 37*
Shadow, 176, 200, 218–220
Shale, 262, 263
SI (International System) measures, R2–R3
Sign language, 14–15
Silver, 156
Simple machines, 108–109, 110*–113, 116–117*, 119–121*, 122–125
Skill builders, 7*, 50*, 82*, 121*, 146*, 178*, 209*, 247*, 273*, 295*, 328*, 367*, 402*, 415*
Skills, using, 7*, 50*, 61, 63, 82*, 125, 127, 146*, 178*, 189, 191, 209*, 247*, 253, 255, 273*, 295*, 317, 319, 328*, 367*, 381, 383, 429, 431
Skin, 386–387*, 388–391, 392*–395, 397*

Slate, 263
Small intestine, 425, 429
Sodium, 158
Sodium chloride, 158
Soil, 39, 165*, 266–267, 290–291*, 292–295*, 296, 384
layers of, 293
properties of, 294
Soil formation, 293
Solar cells, 233
Solar eclipse, 218, 220, 222–224
Solar energy, 360–361
Solar flare, 231
Solar storm, 231
Solar system, 236–240*, 244–245*, 246–247*, 248–251, 253, 256
Solar wind, 250
Solids, 16, 49, 140–141*, 142–143, 145–146*, 147, 150–151, 157, 162
Solution, 148, 162
Sound waves, 180–181
South pole, 197
Space, 131*–132, 137
Space foods, 418–419
Space probe, 238, 242–243, 256
Speed, 67*, 71
Sphere, 205*–206
Spores, 38
Spring scale, 77*–78, R16
Stars, 202–203, 228, 253
Star time, 202–203
Steel, 155*–156
Stomach, 424–425, 429
Stone symbols, 266–267
Stopwatch, R12
Subsoil, 293
Summarizing, 253, 429
Sun, 194–195*, 196–200*, 203, 208, 214, 215*–216,
217*–218, 220–223, 227*–233, 235*, 237*–239, 246, 249, 250, 394–395
Sundial, 199*
Sun's energy, 180–181, 226–227*, 228, 229–231
Sunspots, 229, 231, 253
Survey, 304*
Survival, 362–363*, 364–367*, 368–369, 377–378*
Switch, electrical, 185, 189
System, R19
electrical, 184
Systems of living things, 46, 61

T

Tables, making, 50*, 146*, R23
Tape recorder, R10
Taste buds, 423, 429
Technology in science, 74–75, 172–173, 288–289
Telescope, 240*–241, 253, R9
Temperate forest, 357
Temperature, 166, 227*–228, 281*, 391, R2–R3, R17–R18
Terrace farming, 266–267
Thermometer, 166, 168
Tilted axis, 197–198, 201, 248, 256
Time, 67*, 71, 202–203, 212–213
Tissue, 58, 61
Topsoil, 293
Total eclipse, 220
Trash, 313–314
Triceps, 84–85
Tubers, 38

Tundra – Year

Tundra, 267, 304

U

Ultraviolet light, 394–395
Unbalanced forces, 89
Unequal forces, 89
Uranus, 236–237, 248
Using numbers, 121*
Using observations, 247
Using patterns, 209*
Using variables, 178*

V

Vaccines, 404, 408
Valley, 264–265
Variables, using, 178*, 189
Venus, 236–237, 238

Viruses, 381, 399, 406–408
Vitamins, 414, 429
Volcanic eruption, 372
Volcanoes, 239, 283
Volume, 131*–132, 133, 135, 245*–246, 295*, R2–R3, R13

W

Wastes, 15*, 16, 49, 391, 425
Water, 15*, 158, 165*, 210, 295*, 305, 308–309*, 310–311*, 360–361, 414
Water filtration model, 311*
Water pollution, 308–309*, 310–311*, 316
Water transport system, 58
Water vapor, 145
Water waves, 180–181
Weather, 281
Weathering, 270, 272, 273*–275, 278–279*, 280–281*

Weather satellites, 288–289
Wedge, 119, 125
Weight, 81, 82*, 83, 136, R2–R3, R16
Wetland, 326–327
Wheels, 111–113, 125
White blood cells, 400, 403, 408
Wind energy, 360–361
Windpipe, 428
Work, 98–99*, 100–101*, 106–107*, 108, 110*, 111–113, 116–117*, 118–121*, 122–123, 125

Y

Year, 198

R46   * Indicates an activity related to this topic.

CREDITS

Design & Production: Kirchoff/Wohlberg, Inc.

Maps: Geosystems.

Transvision: Ken Karp (photography); Michael Maydak (illustration).

Illustrations: Ken Batelman p.428; Ka Botzis: pp. 271, 274, 293, 325, 368, 376; Elizabeth Callen: 360; Barbara Cousins: pp. 85, 423, 424, 425; Steve Cowden pp. 350–351; Marie Dauenheimer: pp. 388–389, 390–391, 399, 400–401; Michael DiGiorgio: pp. 328, 335, 339, 364; Jeff Fagan: pp. 12, 58, 88, 89, 91, 101, 102; Lee Glynn: pp. 15, 71, 72, 82, 83, 136, 159, 230, 256, 313, 352, 357, 384, 398, 416, 432; Kristen Goeters: p. 137; Colin Hayes: p. 173 Handbook pp. R7, R11, R13, R20–R23; Nathan Jarvis: pp. 68, 69, 70; Matt Kania: pp. 264, 283; Virge Kask: pp. 14, 26–27; Fiona King: 222, 223. Tom Leonard: pp. 16, 57, 81, 90, 196, 197, 200, 208, 236–237; Olivia: Handbook pp. R2–R4, R9, R10, R13, R16–R19, R21, R23–R25; Sharron O'Neil: pp. 4, 34, 35, 36, 40, 60, 64, 288, 303, 317, 320; Pat Rasch: pp. 79, 80, 118, 119, 120, 121, 128; Rob Schuster: pp. 115, 185, 186, 192, 198–199, 206–207, 216, 218, 219, 244; Casey Shain: p. 304; Wendy Smith: pp. 338, 344, 326–327; Matt Straub: pp. 42, 61, 96, 125, 162, 166, 189, 224, 228, 253, 317, 352, 381, 408, 429; Ted Williams: pp. 154, 156, 167, 178, 182, 184; Jonathan Wright: pp. 110, 111, 113.

Photography Credits:

Contents: iii: Bob & Clara Calhoun/Bruce Coleman, Inc. iv: inset, Bob Winsett/Corbis; FPG. v: Richard Megna/Fundamental Photographs. vi: ESA/Science Photo Library. vii: Roger Werth/Woodfin Camp & Associates, Inc. viii: Gregory Ochocki/Photo Researchers, Inc. ix: Walter Bibikow/FPG.

National Geographic Invitation to Science: S2: Emory Kristof; inset, Harriet Ballard. S3: t. Woods Hole Oceanographic Institution; b. Jonathan Blair.

Be a Scientist: S5: David Mager. S6: NASA. S7: t. Corbis; b, Francois Gohier/Photo Researchers, Inc. S8: l, Jonathan Blair/Woodfin Camp & Associates; r, Wards SCI/Science Source/Photo Researchers, Inc. S11: NASA. S12: John Sanford/Science Photo Library/Photo Researchers, Inc. S13: t, b, NASA. S14: Michael Marten/Science Photo Library/Photo Researchers, Inc. S15: Peter Beck/The Stock Market. S16: l, K. Preuss/The Image Works; r, Richard A. Cooke III/Tony Stone Images. S17: Jean Miele/The Stock Market.

Unit 1: 1: Dieter & Mary Plage/Bruce Coleman, Inc.; Randy Morse/Animals Animals, inset b.r. 2: Richard Nowitz/FPG. 3: Ken Karp. 5: Ken Karp, t.r.; R. Calentine/Visuals Unlimited, b. 6: Barry L. Runk/Grant Heilman, b.l.; Runk/Schoenberger/Grant Heilman, b.r. 7: Ken Karp. 8: Sullivan & Rogers/Bruce Coleman, Inc., t.r.; Tom J. Ulrich/Visuals Unlimited, b.c. 9: Cart Roessler/Animals Animals. 10: Ronald H. Cohn. H. S. Terrence 11: Animals Animals. 13: Ken Karp. 15: Ken Karp. 17: C. Bradley Simmons/Bruce Coleman, Inc., t.r.; Jerry Cooke/Animals Animals. 18: Jim Zipp/Photo Researchers, Inc., c.; Kim Taylor/Bruce Coleman, Inc., r.; Lefever/Grushow/Grant Heilman, l. 19: Arthur Tilley/FPG. 20: Ken Lucas/Visuals Unlimited, l. 20–21: Skip Moody/Dembinsky Photo Assoc. 21: The Blake School, t. 22: Tim Davis/Zipp/Photo Researchers, Inc. 23: Ken Karp. 24: Dwight R. Kuhn, t.l.; Glenn M. Oliver/Visuals Unlimited, t.c.; Pat Lynch/Zipp/Photo Researchers, Inc., t.r.; Robert P. Carr/Bruce Coleman, Inc., b.l. 25: John Mielcarek/Dembinsky Photo Assoc., b.l.; Nuridsany et Perennou/Zipp/Photo Researchers, Inc. t.l.; Robert L. Dunne/Bruce Coleman, Inc., t.r.; Sharon Cummings/Dembinsky Photo Assoc., b.r.. 26: Henry Ausloos/Animals Animals. 28: Debra P. Hershkowitz/Bruce Coleman, Inc., t.l.; Ken Karp, b.r. 29: Rhoda Sidney/PhotoEdit. 30: Bill Banaszewski/Visuals Unlimited, inset. 30–31: J.C. Carton/Bruce Coleman, Inc., bkgrd. 32: Toyohiro Yamada/FPG. 33: Ken Karp. 34: Inga Spence/Visuals Unlimited, t.c.; Patti Murray/Animals Animals, l. 36: George F. Mobley, l. 37: Bill Bachman/Photo Researchers, Inc. 38: D. Cavagnaro/Visuals Unlimited, t.l.; Dwight R. Kuhn, b.r.; Dwight R. Kuhn, b.l.; John Lemker/Animals Animals, b.c.. 39: Larry Lefever/Grant Heilman. 40–41: Randy Green/FPG, bkgrd.; Stan Osolinski/Dembinsky Photo Assoc. inset t.; Larry West/FPG., inset b. 41: John M. Roberts/The Stock Market, inset t.; J. H. Robinson/Photo Researchers, Inc., inset b. 43: Superstock; Peter Cade/Tony Stone Images, inset b.r. 44: PhotoDisc., all. 45: Ken Karp. 46: Rob Gage/FPG. 47: Joe McDonald/Animals Animals, b.r.; John Shaw/Bruce Coleman, Inc., t.r. 48: Leonard Rue III/Visuals Unlimited, b.; Robert P. Carr/Bruce Coleman, Inc., t.l. 49: F.C. Millington-TCL/Masterfile, b.r.; Tom McHugh/Photo Researchers, Inc., t.r. 51: Bonnie Kamin/PhotoEdit. 52: Joyce Photographics/Photo Researchers, Inc., t.; Sonya Jacobs/The Stock Market, l. 53: John D. Cunningham/Visuals Unlimited, r.; John Sohlden/Visuals Unlimited, b.l.; Michael T. Stubben/Visuals Unlimited, t.c.; R.J. Erwin/Photo Researchers, Inc., t.l. 54: Ken Karp. 55: Margaret Oechsli/Fundamental Photographs. 56: Dwight R. Kuhn, t.l.; Ken Karp, b.r. 59: Dennis MacDonald/PhotoEdit. 60: Phillip Hayson/Photo Researchers, Inc.

Unit 2: 65: ZEFA Stock Imagery, Inc. 66: Anderson Monkmeyer, b.l.; Dollarhide/Monkmeyer, b.r. 67: Ken Karp, b.r.; Will Hart/PhotoEdit, t.r.. 69: Ken Karp. 70: Barbara Leslie/FPG, b.r.; K.H. Switak/Photo Researchers, Inc., b.l. 71: K. & K. Amman/Bruce Coleman, Inc./PNI. 73: Jacob Taposchaner/FPG. 74: Dan McCoy/Rainbow/PNI. 75: David Young-Wolff/PhotoEdit. 76: Ken Karp. 77: Ken Karp. 78: Ken Karp. 80: RubberBall Productions. 84: Ken Karp. 86: Ken Karp. 87: Ken Karp. 90: NASA. 91: Ken Karp. 92: Ken Karp. 93: Jade Albert/FPG. 94–95: Stephen J. Shaluta, Jr./Dembinsky Photo Assoc. 95: Ken Karp. 97: Chris Salvo/FPG. 98: Camelot/Photonica, b.r.; Jacob Taposchaner/FPG, b.l.; Will & Deni McIntyre/Photo Researchers, Inc., t.c. 99: Ken Karp. 100: Camelot/Photonica, b.l.; Ken Karp, t.l. & m.l. 101: Ken Karp. 103: R. Hutchings/PhotoEdit. 104–105: Ed Degginger/Bruce Coleman, Inc., bkgrd. 105: Jeff Foott/Bruce Coleman, Inc. b. inset; Jonathan Nourok/PhotoEdit, t. inset. 106: Ken Karp. 107: Ken Karp. 109: Ken Karp. 110: Ken Karp, t. & b. 112: Ken Karp. 114–115: The Granger Collection New York. 116: Carl Purcell/Photo Researchers, Inc. 117: Ken Karp. 118: Dollarhide/Monkmeyer. 119: W. Metzen/Bruce Coleman, Inc. 123: Ken Karp. 124: David Mager.

Unit 3: 129: Bkgrd: MMSD Joe Sohm/ChromoSohm. 130: Ken Karp. 131: Ken Karp. inset 132: PhotoDisc. 133: MMSD, m.r.; PhotoDisc, m.c., b.l. & b.r.; Sylvain Grandadam/Photo Researchers, Inc., t.r. 134: Stockbyte. 135: PhotoDisc, b.l.; Ken Karp, t.r. 138: Robert Rathe/NIST; inset, Joe Sohm/Stock, Boston/PNI. 140: Gerry Ellis/ENP Images. 141: Ken Karp. 142: PhotoDisc. 143: PhotoDisc, b.c. & b.r.; Ken Karp, b.l. 144: Lawrence Migdale, l. & b.m.; Margerin Studio/FPG, t.r. 145: Ken Karp. 146: Peter Scoones-TCL/Masterfile. 147: PhotoDisc. 148: Ken Karp. 149: Arthur Tilley/FPG. 150: McGraw Hill School Division. 150–151: Ken Karp, insets. 152: Ken Karp. 153: Ken Karp. 154: Leonard Lessin/Peter Arnold, Inc. 155: PhotoDisc, t.r.; Ken Karp, b.r. 156: Telegraph Colour Library/FPG. 157: Ken Karp. 158: PhotoDisc. 160: Stan Osolinski/Dembinsky Photo Assoc. Charles D. Winters/Photo Researchers, Inc.161: t. Mehau Kulyk/Photo Researchers, Inc. b. William Waterfall/The Stock Market. 163: Eric Meola/The Image Bank; Tom Bean, inset b.r. 164: Ken Karp. 165: Ken Karp. 168: Ben Simmons/The Stock Market, l.; Eric Gay/AP/World Wide Photos, b.r. 169: Ken Karp. 170: Nakita Ovsyanikov/Masterfile, b.r.; Robert P. Carr/Bruce Coleman, Inc., l. 171: Ken Karp. 172: Culver Pictures, Inc. 172–173: Gary Buss FPG, bkgrd. 174: Ken Karp. 175: Ken Karp. 176: Ron Thomas/FPG. 177: Gary Withey/Bruce Coleman, Inc., b.r.; Jerome Wexler/Photo Researchers, Inc., t.r.; Ken Karp, b.l.; Telegraph Colour Library/FPG, b.c. 179: Tim Davis/Photo Researchers, Inc. 180: Frank Krahmer/Bruce Coleman, Inc., b.l. 181: Telegraph Colour Library/FPG, bkgrd.; Ken Karp, inset. 183: Ken Karp. 188: PhotoDisc bkgrd.; Ken Karp, insets.

Unit 4: 193: NASA/FPG; inset, GSO Images/The Image Bank. 194: George D. Lepp/Photo Researchers, Inc. 195: Ken Karp. 197: Jim Cummins. FPG. 200: Ken Karp. 201: Andy Levin/Photo Researchers, Inc. 202: Michael R. Whelan, inset; Jim Ballard/AllStock/PNI, t. 204–205: Edward R. Degginger/Bruce Coleman, Inc. 205: Ken Karp. 206–207: John Sanford/Science Photo Researchers, Inc. 208–209: NASA. 210: NASA, b.l.; Michael P. Gadomski/Photo Researchers, Inc., t.l. 211: Richard T. Nowitz/Corbis. 212: Chris Dube. 212–213: t. Photo Disc. 213: The Granger Collection New York. 214: Matt Bradley/Bruce Coleman, Inc. 215: Ken Karp. 217: Archive Photos/PNI, b.r.; Ken Karp, b.l. 218: Frank Rossotto/The Stock Market. 219: Rev. Ronald Royer/Photo Researchers, Inc. 220–221: Pekka/Photo Researchers, Inc. 222-223: Visuals Unlimited. 225: Science Photo Library/Photo Researchers, Inc. 226: Mike Yamashita/Woodfin Camp & Associates. 227: Ken Karp. 228: Jerry Schad/Photo Researchers, Inc. 229: Francois Gohier/Photo Researchers, Inc., b.; Jerry Lodriguss/Photo Researchers, Inc., t. 231: Detlev Van/Photo Researchers, Inc., t.; Ken Karp, b. 232: Jim Cummins/FPG. 233: t. NASA/Photo Researchers, Inc. b. Telegraph

R47

Colour Library/FPG 234: Palomar Observatory/Caltech. 235: Ken Karp. 238: NASA/Mark Marten/Photo Researchers, Inc., b.; US Geological/Photo Researchers, Inc., t. 239: NASA/Science Source/Photo Researchers, Inc., b.; US Geological Survey/Photo Researchers, Inc., t. 240: Ken Karp. 241: Mugshots/The Stock Market. 242: A. Ramey Stock Boston, l. NASA/JPL/Corbis; 242–243: USGS/Photo Researchers, Inc., bkgrd. 243: NASA/Corbis, b.r. Photo Researchers, Inc., bkgrd. 245: Ken Karp. 246: Science Photo Library/Photo Researchers, Inc. 247: Ken Karp. 248: NASA, t.; NASA/Mark Marten/Photo Researchers, Inc., b. 249: NASA Science Photo Library/Photo Researchers, Inc., b.; Space Telescope/Photo Researchers, Inc., t. 250–251: Jerry Lodriguss/Photo Researchers, Inc. 251: Nieto/Jerrican/Photo Researchers, Inc. 252: Sam Zarembar/The Image Bank, bkgrd.; The Granger Collection, inset.

Unit 5: 257: ZEFA/Stock Imagery, Inc. 258: PhotoDisc, b.l.; Ann Purcell/Photo Researchers, Inc., b.r.; Jeffrey Myers/FPG, t.r. 259: Ken Karp. 260: Joyce Photographics/Photo Researchers, Inc., b.c.; Ken Karp, t.l., m.l., b.l., b.r. 261: Ken Karp. 262: PhotoDisc, bkgrd.; Ken Karp, insets. 263: l. col. from top, Stephen Ogilvy, Ken Karp, Stephen Ogilvy, E.R. Degginger/Photo Researchers, Inc.; r. col. from top, Stephen Ogilvy, Ken Karp, Ken Karp, Charles R. Belinky/Photo Researchers, Inc. 264: Diane Rawson; Photo Researchers, Inc., b.l.; Josef Beck/FPG, m.l.; Tim Davis/Photo Researchers, Inc, b.r. 265: Yann Arthus-Bertrand/Corbis. 266: Art Wolfe/AllStock/PNI, t.; Robert Harding Picture Library, inset; 267: Fergus O'Brien/FPG International, t.; D. E. Cox/Tony Stone Images, m. 268: Francois Gohier/Photo Researchers, Inc. 269: Ken Karp. 270: Keith Kent/Science/Photo Researchers, Inc., bkgrd.; Susan Rayfield/Photo Researchers, Inc., inset l & r. 271: Ken Karp. 272: Farrell Grehan/Photo Researchers, Inc., t.; Ken M. Johns/Photo Researchers, Inc., b. 273: Ken Karp. 274: Dan Guravich/Photo Researchers, Inc. 275: Ralph N. Barrett/Bruce Coleman, Inc. 276: Adam Jones/Photo Researchers, Inc., t.r.; John Sohlden/Visuals Unlimited, b.r.; W. E. Ruth/Bruce Coleman, Inc., b.l. 276–277: PhotoDisc., bkgrd. 277: The National Archives/Corbis, t.r.; Pat Armstrong/Visuals Unlimited, b.l.; Sylvan H. Wittaver/Visuals Unlimited, t.l. 278: Warren Faidley/International Stock. 279: Ken Karp. 280: NASA/GSFC/Photo Researchers, Inc. 281: PhotoDisc. 282: Paul Sakuma/AP/Wide World Photos, b.; Will & Deni McIntyre/Photo Researchers, Inc., t. 283: PhotoDisc. 284: Arthur Rothstein/AP Photo, b.; Sergio Dorantes, t. 285: The Weather Channel. 286: Jeffrey Howe/Visuals Unlimited. 286–287: Telegraph Colour Library/FPG, bkgrd. 287: Frank Rossotto/The Stock Market, t.r.; NOAA/Science Photo Library/Photo Researchers, Inc., m.r.; Dr. Denise M. Stephenson-Hawk, b.r. 289: PhotoDisc, bkgrd.; Stock Imagery, Inc., inset. 290: PhotoDisc, b.r.; Michael P. Gadomski/Photo Researchers, Inc., b.l.; Peter Skinner/Photo Researchers, Inc., t.r. 291: Ken Karp. 292: Craig K. Lorenz/Photo Researchers, Inc. 294: Ken Karp. 295: Ken Karp. 296: Jim Foster/The Stock Market, b.; M. E. Warren/Photo Researchers, Inc., t. 297: Debra P. Hershkowitz/Bruce Coleman, Inc. 298: The National Archives/Corbis, inset. 298–299: John Elk III/Bruce Coleman, Inc., bkgrd. 299: G. Buttner/Okapia/Photo Researchers, Inc., b.r.; Roy Morsch/The Stock Market, t.r. 300: Liaison Agency, b.r.; Owen Franken/Corbis, b.l. 301: Ken Karp. 302: Phillip Hayson/Photo Researchers, Inc., t.; Richard Hamilton Smith/Corbis., b. 303: Ray Ellis/Photo Researchers, Inc. 304: Will McIntyre/Photo Researchers, Inc. 305: Ken Karp. 306: Bruce Byers/FPG, b.c.; Ken Karp., t.b.l. 306–307: Jeffrey Sylvester/FPG. 307: Norman Owen Tomalin/Bruce Coleman, Inc., r. & b.;Steve Kline/Bruce Coleman, Inc., inset. 308: Lawson Wood/Corbis. 309: Ken Karp. 310: PhotoDisc. 311: Ken Karp. 312: PhotoDisc. b.l. Stuart Cahill/AFP/BETTMAN. 315: PhotoDisc. 316: David Sucsy/FPG bkgrd.; Barbara Comnes, inset.

Unit 6: 321: Craig K. Lorenz/Photo Researchers, Inc., bkgrd; Richard Price/FPG, inset. 322: Renee Lynn/Photo Researchers, Inc. 323: Ken Karp. 324: Gary Randall/FPG, b.; Lee Foster/Bruce Coleman, Inc., t. 329: Jon Feingersh/The Stock Market. 330: George F. Mobley, t.; 1998 Comstock, Inc., inset. 331: Emory Kristof. 332: Tim Davis/Photo Researchers, Inc. 333: Ken Karp. 334: Gary Meszaros/Visuals Unlimited. 336: Farrell Grehan/Photo Researchers, Inc., r. ; Rod Planck/Photo Researchers, Inc., l. 337: Ken Karp. 340–341: clockwise from top: Charles Gold/The Stock Market; Denise Cupen/Bruce Coleman, Inc.; Roy Morsch/The Stock Market. Don Mason/The Stock Market; Ed Bock/The Stock Market; Elaine Twichell/Dembinsky Photo Assoc.; J. Barry O'Rourke/The Stock Market; J Sapinsky/The Stock Market; Rex A. Butcher/Bruce Coleman, Inc. 340–341: Telegraph Colour/FPG. 342: Ken Karp. 343: Ken Karp. 345: Dennie Cody/FPG, l; DiMaggio/Kalish/The Stock Market, r. 346: Paul A. Zahl, l; William E. Townsend/Photo Researchers, Inc., r. 347: Arthur Norris/Visuals Unlimited, l.; Biophoto Associates/Photo Researchers, Inc., r. 348: Ken Karp, b.; Zig Leszcynski/Animals Animals, t. 349: Lynwood Chase/Photo Researchers, Inc. 353: Gil Lopez-Espina/Visuals Unlimited, inset; K & K Ammann/Bruce Coleman, Inc., bkgrd. 354: Michael Gadomski/Photo Researchers, Inc. 355: Ken Karp. 356: Joe McDonald/Bruce Coleman, Inc., t.; John Shaw/Bruce Coleman, Inc., b. 358: Ken Karp. 359: Kenneth W. Fink/Bruce Coleman, Inc. 361: Ken Lucas/Visuals Unlimited. 362: Richard Kolar/Animals Animals, l.; Richard & Susan Day/Animals Animals, b. 363: Ken Karp. 365: Barbara Gerlach/Visuals Unlimited, t.; Zefa Germany/The Stock Market, b. 366: A. Cosmos Blank/Photo Researchers, Inc., b.l.; Breck P. Kent/Animals Animals, t.; Robert P. Carr/Bruce Coleman, Inc., b.r. 367: Ken Karp. 369: Emily Stong/Visuals Unlimited. 370: Art Wolfe/Tony Stone Images t.c.; Tom Brakefield/The Stock Market, b. 371: Gerald & Buff Corsi/Visuals Unlimited, t.l.; Stephen Dalton/Photo Researchers, Inc., t.r.; Dan Suzio/Photo Researchers, Inc., b. 372: David Weintraub/Photo Researchers, Inc. 373: Ken Karp. 374: Keith Gunnar/Bruce Coleman, Inc., l.; Phil Degginger/Bruce Coleman, Inc., r. 375: Pat & Tom Leeson/Photo Researchers, Inc. 376: Joe McDonald/Visuals Unlimited. 377: Joe & Carol McDonald/Visuals Unlimited. 378: Ken Karp., b.; Omikron/Photo Researchers, Inc., t. 379: Pat & Tom Leeson/Photo Researchers, Inc. 380: Photo Disc t.; Janis Burger/Bruce Coleman, Inc., t.r.; Jen and Des Bartlett/Bruce Coleman, Inc., b.l.; Tom Van Sant/The Stock Market, bkgrd.

Unit 7: 385: George Schiavone/The Stock Market. 386: Gary Landsman/The Stock Market. 387: Ken Karp. 388: Yoav Levy/Phototake. 389: Barbara Peacock/FPG. 392: Ken Karp. 393: Ken Karp. 394: Michael Townsend/Tony Stone Images, t.; Randy Taylor/Liaison Agency, inset; 395: Bob Daemmrich/The Image Works. 396: David Waldorf/FPG. 397: Ken Karp. 399: David M. Phillips/Visuals Unlimited. 401: Manfred Kage/Peter Arnold, Inc. 402: Ken Karp. 403: Mary Kate Denny/PhotoEdit. 404: CORBIS/BETTMANN–UPI. 405: Sandy Fox/MMSD. 406: Howard Sochurek/The Stock Market, inset; Deborah Gilbert/The Image Bank, b. 407: Telegraph Colour Library/FPG, bkgrd. r. McGraw Hill School Division. 409: Otto Rogge/The Stock Market; t. Tracy/FPG. 410: Joyce Photographics/Photo Researchers, Inc., l.; Steven Needham/Envision, r. 411: Ken Karp. 412–413: Ken Karp. 414: David Young-Wolff/PhotoEdit, t.; Ken Karp, b. 417: Michael Newman/PhotoEdit. 418: NASA/Photri, b.r. & m.r. 419: NASA/Photri, t.r., m.r. & b.r.; NASA/Corbis, inset top. 418–419: Ronald Royer/Photo Researchers, Inc. 420: David Young-Wolff/PhotoEdit. 421: Ken Karp. 422: Michael A. Keller/The Stock Market. 426: Ken Karp. 428: Bkgrd: PhotoDisc.

Handbook: Steven Ogilvy: pp. R6, R8, R12, R14, R15, R26.